Praise for *Any Dumb-Ass Can Do It*

"Garry Ridge is the embodiment of what it means to be a great CEO. That he took the time to write down how he learned to lead (with such humility, I might add) means that we all get to learn how to lead like him. And that can only be a good thing!"

—Simon Sinek, Optimist and *New York Times* Bestselling Author,
Start with Why and *The Infinite Game*

"It's not every day that you come across a CEO who aims to be the dumbest person in the room. Garry Ridge's take on leadership is as refreshing as it is rare."

—Adam Grant, #1 *New York Times* Bestselling Author,
Think Again and *Hidden Potential*, and Host, *WorkLife* podcast

"The most useful, fun, and B.S.-free book I have ever read by a veteran CEO. I loved every page, as Garry Ridge's warmth, wisdom, and humor made it such a joy to read. And the simple but powerful advice packed into every chapter sticks with me. I am especially fond of 'What If Your Workplace Was Where People Escaped *To*?' and 'Even the Queen Sits Down to Pee.'"

—Robert I. Sutton, Stanford Professor Emeritus, and *New York Times*
Bestselling Author, *The No Asshole Rule* and *The Friction Project* (with Huggy Rao)

"I absolutely *loved* this book. Garry Ridge wants you to know that being a great leader is simple. Any dumb-ass can do it. But simple, alas, doesn't mean easy. Becoming a great leader means becoming a better person—more caring, curious, and humble, and more fully dedicated to making things better. In delightful page after page, Garry delightfully conveys the accumulated stories and wisdom of decades of leadership practice. Better yet, each of the book's short, readable, and inspiring chapters end with immediately actionable advice."

—Amy C. Edmondson, Novartis Professor of Leadership, Harvard Business School,
and Author, *Right Kind of Wrong: The Science of Failing Well*

"With his characteristic storytelling flair (and occasionally irreverent humor), Garry Ridge distills decades of experience into a powerful, no-nonsense guide that challenges conventional leadership paradigms. At the center of Ridge's vision is the idea of servant-leadership, the idea that by focusing on helping others, we can create thriving organizations where people feel safe, supported, and empowered. A must-read for anyone aspiring to lead with both heart and integrity."

—Hubert Joly, former CEO, Best Buy; Senior Lecturer, Harvard Business School;
and Bestselling Author, *The Heart of Business*

"Garry Ridge has crafted a leadership guide that is both refreshingly candid and deeply insightful in *Any Dumb-Ass Can Do It*. He shares the pivotal moments that shaped his journey, proving that great leadership isn't about being the smartest person in the room, but about genuinely caring for people and learning from every experience. This book is a testament to the power of simple yet profound actions that can transform not just a workplace, but lives. Whether you're at the beginning of your leadership path or a seasoned executive, Garry's wisdom will resonate and inspire you to lead with authenticity, empathy, and a commitment to making others happy. This is a must-read for anyone who believes in the importance of building a positive, people-centered culture."

—Marshall Goldsmith, *Thinkers50* #1 Executive Coach
and *New York Times* Bestselling Author, *The Earned Life, Triggers,*
and *What Got You Here Won't Get You There*

"This book is like getting personal letters from an experienced and accomplished leader. It's got deep insights in leaders in a conversational, and sometimes even comical, style. Garry outlines how to be the leader everyone wants to follow. . . just by being yourself."

—David Burkus, Bestselling Author, *Best Team Ever*

"Garry Ridge is one of the great unsung CEOs of our generation. In his typically humble way, he's sharing his best insights on what's made WD-40 an extraordinary company. And the good news is that you don't need to be a dumb-ass; you just need to read the book."

—Michael Bungay Stanier, Author, *The Coaching Habit* and *The Advice Trap*

"These days, lots of former CEOs are getting on the bandwagon and codifying their careers into wisdom for the world. Some are great, and some, well, mere vanity books. But the book you are holding is a veritable treasure trove of guidance and wisdom you will repeatedly return to. This is as close as you'll get to a coffee shop chat with Garry, as he has vulnerably and courageously given us a personal tour of his storied career, and drenched us in practical, caring guidance every leader will be grateful to apply. Those you lead will be cheering as they watch you transform putting these insights into practice. Read it slowly. Twice."

—Ron Carucci, Managing Partner, Navalent, and Bestselling,
Award-Winning Author, *Rising to Power* and *To Be Honest*

"The best thing you can do is take a moment to learn from Garry Ridge, one of the best leaders, hands down, I've met! The worst thing you can do is not lose yourself in his wise and utterly charming stories. And the first thing you should do is pick up this book. Now!"

—Whitney Johnson, CEO, Disruption Advisors; Global Top 10 Management Thinker,
Thinkers50; *Wall Street Journal* Bestselling Author, *Disrupt Yourself* and *Smart Growth*

"In *Any Dumb-Ass Can Do It*, Garry Ridge masterfully reveals the secrets behind WD-40's extraordinary culture. His insights offer a blueprint for any leader seeking to foster innovation, loyalty, and a friction-free culture. This book is a must-read for anyone looking to transform their team or entire organization into a thriving, cohesive tribe."

—Adrian Gostick & Chester Elton, *New York Times* Bestselling Authors,
Anxiety at Work, The Carrot Principle, and *Leading with Gratitude*

"If there were an Olympic event for culture building, Garry Ridge would be wearing a gold medal around his neck. He's lived it, breathed it, made it happen, and reached the top of the rostrum .. for real. Now he's written down in *Any Dumb-Ass Can Do It* the leadership lessons he's learned from decades of putting in the hard work. This book is vintage Garry— irreverent, soulful, passionate, honest, practical, funny, and full of great stories. And there's also great joy in this book. There's a profound sense you get when reading *Any Dumb-Ass Can Do It* that Garry loves what he does and loves the people he does it with. If you want to learn how to build and sustain an engaging and purposeful organizational culture, you must read this book and then put to work the lessons *you* learn. But, as Garry will tell you, 'It's simple but not easy.' Good on ya, Garry!"

—Jim Kouzes, Coauthor, *The Leadership Challenge*,
and Fellow, Doerr Institute for New Leaders, Rice University

"If you are looking for a book with more substance than fluff to help in your professional development, *Any Dumb-Ass Can Do It* is it! Ridge serves up a highly relatable blueprint to help any leader learn from the moments in their leadership journey and build thriving cultures in the process!"

—Heather R. Younger, JD, CSP, Bestselling Author, *The Art of Caring Leadership*,
The Art of Active Listening, and *The Art of Self-Leadership*

"By every metric I can think of, Garry Ridge was one of the most effective CEOs in the last 50 years. In this fun, engaging book, he makes it clear that truly anyone competent enough to be promoted to a leadership role can realize similar success. And he shares practical, actionable wisdom in bite-size learning moments that help leaders make it happen."

—Matt Tenney, Bestselling Author, *Inspire Greatness*

"A brilliant blend of wit and wisdom, *Any Dumb-Ass Can Do It* proves you don't need to be a genius—just a thoughtful leader who genuinely cares. It's a powerful reminder that true leadership is about connection, authenticity, and showing up fully for your team."

—Morag Barrett, CEO, SkyeTeam, and Award-Winning Author,
You, Me, We; *Cultivate*; and *The Future-Proof Workplace*

"A must-read! Garry Ridge tells the story of how he helped grow WD-40 Company into one of the world's most recognized and trusted brands. In this practical guide you'll discover unexpected and invaluable lessons from a CEO who is world-renowned for creating a high-performing and values-driven culture. A masterclass from a proven leader!"

—Siobhán McHale, Chief Human Resources Officer, DuluxGroup,
and Author, *The Hive Mind at Work* and *The Insider's Guide to Culture Change*

Also by Garry Ridge

Helping People Win at Work: A Business Philosophy Called "Don't Mark My Paper, Help Me Get an A" (with Kenneth Blanchard)

The Unexpected Learning Moment: Lessons in Leading a Thriving Culture Through Lockdown 2020 (with Martha Finney)

Work Is Love Made Visible: A Collection of Essays About the Power of Finding Your Purpose from the World's Greatest Thought Leaders (contributor)

Also by Martha Finney

Best Worst First: 75 Network Marketing Experts on Everything You Need to Know to Build the Business of Your Dreams (with Margie K. Aliprandi)

Building High-Performance People and Organizations

Healing at Work: A Guide to Using Career Conflicts to Overcome Your Past and Build the Future You Deserve (with Susan Schmitt Winchester)

HR from the Heart: Inspiring Stories and Strategies for Building the People Side of Great Business (with Libby Sartain)

Rebound: A Proven Plan for Starting Over After Job Loss

The Truth About Getting the Best from People: Ditch the Carrot and the Stick

Unlock the Hidden Job Market: 6 Steps to a Successful Job Search When Times Are Tough (with Duncan Mathison)

ANY DUMB-ASS CAN DO IT

GARRY RIDGE
and MARTHA FINNEY

MATT HOLT

Matt Holt Books
An Imprint of BenBella Books, Inc.
Dallas, TX

Any Dumb-Ass Can Do It copyright © 2025 by Garry Ridge

Matt Holt is an imprint of BenBella Books, Inc.
8080 N. Central Expressway
Suite 1700
Dallas, TX 75206
benbellabooks.com
Send feedback to feedback@benbellabooks.com

BenBella and *Matt Holt* are federally registered trademarks.

Printed in the United States of America
10 9 8 7 6 5 4 3 2 1

Library of Congress Control Number: 2024039028
ISBN 9781637746295 (hardcover)
ISBN 9781637746301 (electronic)

Editing by Katie Dickman
Copyediting by Michael Fedison
Proofreading by Lisa Story and Becky Maines
Text design and composition by Jordan Koluch
Cover design by Brigid Pearson
Printed by Lake Book Manufacturing

To all the future generations of my family, which began with my mum and dad drinking tea at their kitchen table in Five Dock.

And to all the Dumb-Ass believers who are brave enough to know it's not all about them. It's about those they have the privilege to lead.

Contents

"IF YOU CAN'T MAKE THEM HAPPY, AT LEAST DON'T HURT THEM"

CHEERS, MATE!

If you want to improve,
be content to be thought foolish and stupid.

EPICTETUS

Foreword

More than 20 years ago, my wife, Margie, and I started a Master of Science in Executive Leadership (MSEL) graduate program in cooperation with the University of San Diego. Garry Ridge had just arrived in the United States from Australia to take over as president of WD-40 Company. He thought this program would be particularly helpful to him as he began his role as the company's leader.

During Garry's time in the MSEL program, Margie and I got to know him personally. Soon our relationship grew beyond the classroom, and we became colleagues, coauthors, and great friends.

What I love about *Any Dumb-Ass Can Do It* is the key message that is embedded in every chapter. There is an essential ingredient for creating and leading an organizational culture in which people can thrive—a safe, supportive environment where they can do what they love. It is this: *We must first* **become** *the kind of leader who is willing to do everything it takes to create and lead such a culture.*

This philosophy is grounded in what we commonly recognize as *servant leadership*. Most of us see only the results of a servant leadership approach to leadership: how leaders behave and how their community benefits from those behaviors. But, in truth, servant leadership is an inside-out mindset. It has to start on the inside, with the heart—your character and intentions—who you are as a person, regardless of your official role as a leader. It then moves to the head—your beliefs and attitudes about leadership. Finally, the hands—your actions and behaviors. When your heart and head are right, who you are and what you believe about leadership align with your actions. This convergence demonstrates to the outside world that you have become a servant leader. Garry Ridge is the embodiment of servant leadership.

How did he *become* a servant leader? Through a series of transformative Learning Moments, which he describes in these pages.

Here's my own *becoming* story. In 1977, after I became a tenured professor at the University of Massachusetts, Margie and I went to California for sabbatical leave. During our time there, I was asked to speak at a Young Presidents' Organization (YPO) international university event. I gave a speech about leadership, motivation, and managing change. It was a big hit. After my speech, several YPO members came up to Margie and me and asked about our future plans. We told them we planned to return to Amherst after our sabbatical.

"Oh no, you don't," they said. "You're going to stay in San Diego and start your own company!"

We laughed and said, "We can't even balance our own checkbook. How are we going to start a company?"

But five YPO members promised to be part of an advisory board that would help us with the nuts and bolts of starting our own business. And 45 years later? We're still here.

Our company's flagship leadership training program—which the world knows as simply SLII®—proves this point: When setting a new goal, everyone starts at the developmental stage we call *Enthusiastic Beginner*. They don't know what they are doing (low to zero competence), but they are really excited (high commitment). In order to get to the next phase of development—and the next and then the next—they must be ready, willing, and able to learn. When we met Garry, he was more than willing to learn—from people with experience and expertise, from reading all the books he could get his hands on, and from life experiences he would have along the road to success.

I used to say my teaching goal was to take the BS out of the behavioral sciences. Garry loved that idea and has been doing it ever since. This book brings that thinking alive. When you read it, you'll realize that you can decide what kind of leader you'll be in the future and how you're going to make a difference with your people, your family, and your community.

Thanks, Garry, for growing and *becoming* the leader who continues to inspire us all and make us proud!

Ken Blanchard
Escondido, California

G'DAY, MATE!

Chapter 1

HEY! ARE YOU OKAY?

Epiphanies—which I call *Learning Moments*—come when you least expect them. You can try with all your might to gin up perspective-changing flashes of insight upon command. But it never works that way, does it? The best you can hope for is to have paper, pen, or smartphone at the ready to grab the great revelation before it flies away to find a more receptive mind with the talent of retention and implementation. If that's you, quick! Grab the nugget of wisdom before it gets away!

Fortunately, I had the chance to write mine down. My axis-tilting insight came in a remarkable setting on an otherwise ordinary night on yet another business trip. This time I was flying home to Sydney, Australia, where I could also squeeze in a visit to my mum, who had just passed the 85-year-old milestone. At the moment, I was still in my seat, facing southward—just like my fellow passengers, isolated from each other by our noise-cancelling headphones—into a night sky, leaving San Diego far behind us in the dark.

Ahead of us, just off the horizon still, above our heads, forward of the cockpit, so the pilots would see it first, would eventually loom the Southern Cross—that constellation improbably made famous in the rock song by Crosby, Stills & Nash. Below us thrived all manner of sea life going about its daily business with no thought to the planes flying high overhead. Sharks. Sea turtles. Starfish. Octopus. And, as we closed in on the shallower waters slapping the shores of Sydney, eventually there would be barramundi, wobbegongs, dugongs, and a clever little fellow in the reefs enchantingly called the diagonal-banded sweetlips.

And, of course, there would be dolphins and whales, lounging in their half-brain sleep just under the moon-sparkling surface of the black Pacific Ocean, releasing air bubbles toward the starry sky.

As I was reading an article by the Dalai Lama, and speeding toward the text that contained the life-changing epiphany as assuredly as the jet was speeding toward our destination, my fellow passengers were releasing thoughts into the air, like bubbles from the sleeping whales below. Assuming the passengers were a fair representation of working people from all around the world, over two-thirds of them were sending the same thought up into the night sky:

I hate my job.

So, what was in the article that changed the course of the way I would live out the purpose of my own career? Just two simple sentences. Because it was by the Dalai Lama, of course those sentences would be to the point, precisely *because* of their simplicity:

"Our prime purpose in life is to make others happy. And if we can't make them happy, at least don't hurt them."

With that flash of insight, I could feel around me the suffering and frustration of disenfranchised fellow human beings, all of us headed for the same destination, Australia. Setting aside the holiday travelers, who, presumably, were excited about their vacation choice, the remaining were most likely traveling because of their work. And many of those were hurting.

I had just been promoted into my new role as CEO of WD-40 Company. My job was to not hurt those who came to work every day to build the future for the blue and yellow can with the little red top. My job was to make them happy. But what exactly would that mean over time? Decision after decision? Action after action? Assumption after assumption? None of us intentionally hurt each other (at least I'd like to think that's the case). There has to be more to this business of making each other happy in deep, transcendent ways, starting with taking a serious look at why so many people all over the world hate their jobs. What could I do to make things different at WD-40 Company?

I didn't know it then, primarily because I had not yet developed the words for it nor had the necessary experience of the concept in action, but I was having what I would eventually call a *Learning Moment*—which, as it would turn out, would itself be at the heart of creating a company culture where people were happy, not hurt.

Simply put, I define the Learning Moment as "A positive or negative outcome of any situation that needs to be openly and freely shared to benefit all."

When you break down the concept of the Learning Moment into its essential parts, you'll see that the experience can be either one with a happy ending or an undesirable one. There is no shame in trying something—*wholeheartedly*, as Brené Brown would say—and failing. There is learning; learning that the whole community would benefit from hearing about. In this environment, it would be safe. Safe to innovate. Safe to try and fall short. Safe to succeed, knowing that their colleagues would sincerely celebrate the win. Safe to go and do and then come back and talk about it. Come what may.

But there is an even richer undercurrent to the concept of the Learning Moment. When people feel free to try, fail, and then report back to their colleagues, they are breathing life into the idea of a tribal culture where the members are there to develop, support, feed, and protect one another. Fear would be removed. And in its place would be the feeling of belonging. Of being seen. Thought about. Needed.

Happy.

There's that word again.

There's also the word *happy* that often appears in the Dalai Lama's comments about our purpose in life. He has said, "I believe that the very purpose of life is to be happy. From the very core of our being, we desire contentment. In my own limited experience, I have found that the more we care for the happiness of others, the greater is our own sense of well-being."

Very rapidly I discovered that my purpose as a leader was to make people happy. The experience of being helped would be one of the many facets of the feeling of happiness that governed the WD-40 Company culture.

But is it the company's job to make our people *happy*? And if so, how? That's a topic that has been argued about for decades. Will a new margarita machine really do the trick? How fast would that signing bonus be spent on forgotten luxuries? Would season tickets to the San Diego Padres tweak the engagement scores a point or two in the right direction? What about those who don't like baseball? What do we do to show that we care about them and their happiness?

The C-suite is not a big circus tent with fun and games for boys and girls of all ages. Nobody—especially the employees (or *tribe members*, as they're called at WD-40 Company)—expects to thrive on the sugar high of special events. Although, make no mistake, there's nothing better than a team trip to a Padres game, especially when we're celebrating a big win at work.

Happiness is not about the prizes, the gimmicks, the bonuses. It's about authentic connection that can only be achieved and expressed one way—authentic caring. Not only being seen but also seeing. Not only being helped, but also helping. Mattering. Belonging.

OUR PRIME PURPOSE IN LIFE IS TO MAKE PEOPLE HAPPY

I'm writing this in 2024, four years since the Covid lockdown. We're still trying to make sense of, and pull the lasting wisdom from, all that we learned during that time. One of the cultural eccentricities that emerged was our fondness for telling stories online about how strangers reveal their true character by the way they treat each other in public spaces. They were sort of like digital versions of those ancient cave paintings found in France. We were all stuck in our respective caves. So we occupied some of our time by covering our digital walls with the stories we liked best.

Most of them are likely to be untrue. But we sure did love to share them, didn't we? Each tale expressed our own personal philosophy about life and the intrinsic nature of humanity. Are we mean? Selfish? Rude? Bigoted? Plenty of stories to paint those pictures. Or are we kind? Generous? Self-sacrificing people who stop to notice that the person next to us needs our help? Plenty of stories to paint those pictures too.

My favorite story about human nature is unlikely to be true. But I believe its essence to be accurate. It goes something like this . . .

An anthropology student once asked Margaret Mead what she believed to be the first sign of civilization. The class, trying to anticipate her answer, imagined tools for getting essential survival things done. Or maybe a kitchen midden, a prehistoric treasure trove of thrown-away garbage. Instead of wasted Ziploc bags that could have been run through the dishwasher at least one more time, archeologists have found piles of more basic, but utilitarian, stuff that had clearly been discarded as waste—seashells, stone implements, bones from a long-ago celebration after a particularly skillful hunt. What made them noteworthy was the *collection* of these things, which indicated that a collection of people put them there.

So that was the classroom guess. Made sense. But they were wrong.

As the story is told, Mead said, "A broken human bone. A femur to be precise, which is the thigh bone, which, incidentally, we all need for walking. Therefore, survival in prehistoric times. And not just any femur, but a femur that had been mended."

Historic graveyards are replete with broken human bones. So what's the big deal about this one? The fact that the bone was mended indicated that this particular prehistoric individual had friends. A tribe paused to care for their debilitated companion whose injury could have hobbled the entire group.

In a disparate collection of individualized individuals, no one is stopping to notice—or even care—that someone is suffering. That would impact their performance. And that bison over there will get away. But, assuming the story is true, somewhere along the line the individuals had coalesced into a tribe who cared about each other.

So, whether the story is true or not, I stand by the principle that civilization began when someone stopped, turned around, noticed a struggle, a slowing down, a grimace of pain, and then said,

"Hey! You okay?" And then paused to help. And in the helping, one can only assume there was healing. And in the healing, happiness emerged. Through the safety of belonging, someone was cared for and protected.

As for me, banging around my Australian childhood neighborhood of Five Dock (a suburb just outside of Sydney), no one would have had me pegged as a philosopher princeling or even an anthropologist. I was just a kid who financed my shenanigans by taking the kinds of jobs available to willing children in those days—a newspaper route, and later, a shopkeeper's assistant. If I had had a resume in those days (granted, an unlikely scenario), it would have listed my ever-growing collection of skills and responsibilities as a succession of adults concluded that I could be entrusted with the next new responsibility.

But in retrospect, the most valuable learning would not have appeared on the CV. I was learning that I was creating a place for myself in my community by making others happy. And I must have been learning about how great it felt to be helpful and needed because I still remember those incidents when my young self was desperately needed by the people I worked for. Like the elderly, solitary lady on my newspaper route who always welcomed me with a bag of candy. The pause in our respective days for a brief chat on her stoop kept her loneliness at bay. Or the time when the shop owner received a devastating phone call about a death in his family. He tossed me the keys to the business and raced out the door, leaving me in charge of his entire life's work for days—enough time that I could make a significant difference, for good or ill. I could have preened with pride that he trusted me with the Open sign on the front door. But the most lasting meaning from that moment, as the keys flew through the air toward my open hand, was the fact that

I was *helping* this man cope with a most traumatic family event of grief and tragedy.

Those were my first Learning Moments. Helping others. Making them happy.

WE ARE ALL DUMB-ASSES ON THIS PLANE

I humbly appreciate being recognized for the part I've played in making WD-40 Company the success that it is today, with one of the most beloved brands on the planet.

When I'm asked how I did it, and how others can learn from my example, I just have to respond with, "Any dumb-ass can do it." It's simple but not easy.

I'm just a former newspaper delivery boy, shopkeeper's assistant, DJ, traveling salesman from Five Dock who seemed to make his way through the world with two simple questions: "Hey! You okay?" followed by, "How can I help make you happy?"

And then the Learning Moments came flooding in.

If we keep our mind, eyes, and ears open, every day brings little insights that sparkle and make us just a little wiser, a little bit better, as leaders. But those Learning Moments I'm talking about create big shifts, even with the leverage of the smallest insights, in the most inconsequential episodes of our lives. Like an airplane ride through the dark southern sky.

The result? A culture where people feel safe to try, fail, succeed. To pause to help each other. To ride the inevitable storms together. To celebrate each other's wins. To enjoy being happy together.

To love their jobs.

INTRODUCING THE DUMB-ASS QUICK-START GUIDE

Authors' Note: Too many books on leadership leave readers wondering, "Well, that's all very nice, but what do I do now?" How do you take action to convert the new distinction into new behaviors that will really make a positive difference in your career and workplace culture? We've got you covered! At the end of every chapter, we've included three immediately actionable changes you can (or shouldn't) make to get yourself started. They are:

- The **best** thing you can do.
- The **worst** thing you could do.
- And the **first** thing you should do.

To keep things moving along at a snappy pace, we've simply listed them as Best, Worst, First.

BEST: Remember that as a leader your job is to watch out for and support your people's well-being.

WORST: Assume that because you're the leader, your wish is their command, no matter the cost to their own happiness and sense of value in the workplace.

FIRST: Resolve to learn from the wisest guides and thought leaders.

Chapter 2

YOUR TRIBAL CULTURE IS YOUR MOST ENDURING UNIFIER

This isn't false modesty; it's just the truth. I've got a great face for radio, which turned out to be a good thing for me in the 1980s when I was a disc jockey for a Sydney radio station for which, with my brother Les, we aired a Sunday morning show. I'm not ugly or anything like that. Just not especially remarkable looking. If we were to pass on the sidewalk, you wouldn't look twice. Just an ordinary bloke. Maybe with a nice, friendly smile sent in your direction that lifts your spirits for just a moment, before you pass me by without any more thought.

Unless, of course, I'm with Max the Wonder Dog, my black Lab rescue. In which case, I guarantee you, you'll stop me. And we'll talk about what a good boy he is. And I will agree with you that I'm indeed very lucky to have him. And that's when you'll notice it. *He's not from around here*, you'll think. It's the accent. That accent! Ah yes, Australian.

With that one distinction, I will stand apart from everyone else you will run across that day. Maybe the entire month. Maybe a year. The idea of Australia is immediately inserted into your mind, along with all the cultural attributes you might know about it. Well, kangaroos, for starters. Shrimps and sheilas. The sight of the Sydney Harbour Bridge being the first to televise the celebration fireworks every New Year. Crocodile Dundee and Steve Irwin. Let's see, what else? Nicole Kidman and Hugh Jackman. Bondi Beach, maybe? Uluru (you likely know it better as Ayers Rock), definitely, likely aglow with the sunset. The indigenous Australians, of course, and their haunting didgeridoo.

The eye-popping haka. Naw, mate, that's New Zealand. But we love it too. See? There's something else we have in common!

And above it all, our famous, relaxed friendliness. Spend time with us, you'll not only like us but you'll love yourself more too. That's just the way we are. It's the nature of our tribe. All of these cultural characteristics are universally recognized, and they will flood your brain the second you hear me say, "G'day."

You and I now belong to each other too. We have new attributes in common. We belong to each other, even if it's just in the smallest possible way. Our shared attribute? Well, Max, of course. He remembers you too. You're part of *his* tribe. Why? Well, because you saw what a good boy he is, and even said so out loud. You now officially belong. And we belong to you. We are connected. And the next time we meet on the street, we would say, "Hey! I know you!" Because we belong to each other through our shared experience from before. We recognize each other's attributes. And we know that we are safe in each other's company.

We leaders know a lot about attributes, mostly *brand* attributes. Assuming you've done your due diligence, you know what your customers can reliably expect from your product or service in terms of performance, reliability, consistency, customer service, even the colors on the package. And, if you're a really good leader, you can also describe your *employment attributes*—more commonly known as the *employee value proposition*—those experiences, expectations, treatment, and development opportunities that your people can reliably expect from their leaders (or, as WD-40 Company leaders say, their *coaches*).

What about the *cultural attributes* within the community of all the people who are closely associated with your company? What can they expect from each other as an entire community throughout the various levels of the organization? Those are the attributes that make up the experience that we at WD-40 Company came to call *a tribe*.

The concept of tribe was very much on my mind in my earliest years of leading WD-40 Company, initially as head of the international expansion program and then, three years later, as CEO. My mandate was to expand what was mostly a US-based domestic product with a few small markets elsewhere into a major, globally beloved brand. Eventually the task would be to connect customers in far-flung markets throughout the planet with the experience of using the WD-40 Company products to successfully get the results they needed. "Positive, lasting memories," as we would come to say as our mission.

But first, we had to find ways to create an inspiring, emotionally compelling internal culture within WD-40 Company headquarters that could then be expanded to reach all the global touchpoints. I also had to ask myself what my role would be in this endeavor as the leader. This definitely wasn't the time for a command-and-control attitude. It would have to be more about making people feel invited to a vision that they would want to join. Where they felt safe, supported, welcome, even celebrated, among friends.

To be fair, the WD-40 Company culture as it was when I arrived in San Diego was absolutely appropriate for what it had been until that point. With the exception of a small presence in Australia, Asia, Canada, and the United Kingdom, WD-40 Company was very much a US-based company, with a US-based market of dealers, distributors, and customers. All the emotional connections, esprit de corps, and bonding experiences naturally happened in our small San Diego headquarters. Those of us out there on the other side of the Pacific Ocean were afterthoughts. We didn't take it personally. That was just the way it was. After all, if you're looking for someone to have a spur-of-the-moment lunch with, you're going to pop your head into the office next door. Not ask the guy 7,500 miles away if he's game for a quick bite. He's likely to be asleep anyway.

But now my mandate was to grow WD-40 Company into a *global* company, eventually building a strong presence and loyal following in 176 countries. Strong, enduring, healthy relationships around the planet would be forged.

THE ESSENTIAL COMPONENTS
FOR A FLOURISHING TRIBE

All the press releases or investor relations campaigns in the world weren't going to force that transformation into reality. We had to start with the people of WD-40 Company. We had to define unifying attributes that *everyone* could enthusiastically align themselves with, where the country leader in France confidently knows he or she belongs to the company as much as the sales director in San Diego.

How do we unify a rapidly growing and transforming company to embrace a wide variety of cultures and economic/market variables the world over? Along with my studies and wise personal mentoring from such experts as Ken Blanchard, I became inspired by the tribal cultures all over the world throughout the centuries. I even sat down with Fijian tribal leaders to absorb their wisdom. And, of course, most specifically, the tribal culture of the indigenous Australians in my native homeland.

This model of cohesiveness could be applied to the workplace, and its components would ignite resilience, trust, teamwork, and faith in the future that would prevail, no matter what the external conditions might be at the present moment. Those were the cultural attributes that I wanted to carry WD-40 Company into its new iteration as a beloved, global brand. It would start with a beloved tribe. Those were the characteristics of the WD-40 culture that would enable tribe members all over the world to encounter each other and be able to say right from the start, "Hey, I know you!"

Among my first discoveries was this wonderful definition of a tribe by author Sebastian Junger, in his book *Tribe: On Homecoming and Belonging*: "The earliest and most basic definition of community—of tribe—would be the group of people that you both help feed and help defend." Then I expanded the definition to read this way: "A tribe is a group of people who come together to protect and feed each other; who are dedicated to learning and teaching; who have a set of compelling values that protect them and set them free; who respect people who have different specialized skills. They're a group of people who are focused on the future, because we're going to be looking to where our next horizon of growth around the world is. We celebrate what we do."

That is about as all-encompassing and mutually dependent as anyone could expect from a collection of individuals who are intrinsically entwined with each other's fates and futures. But who started out as strangers at the first day on the job. With that definition as my North Star, and with the help of others much wiser than I, I then identified the following seven essential components that must exist within the tribe for it to flourish long after its chieftain (or CEO) has been replaced, with that replacement in turn replaced by another and eventually another. The tribe remains and prevails deep into a future that resides far beyond our ability to even imagine.

Learning and Teaching

How do we know how to feed and defend ourselves (and, by extension, each other)? Through the skills we have acquired along the way. How are these skills acquired? Someone patiently teaches us. The indigenous Australians of my native Australia aren't born knowing how to bring down a kangaroo for its meat. They are taught by elders who know that their ultimate role is to give the tribe what it needs to thrive throughout future generations. It's not a matter of "will you please hurry up and learn this already?" It's "whatever it takes to teach you this skill so you can contribute to the long-term success of our tribe . . . and eventually pass it on to future hunters, yet to be born. While you learn what I'm teaching you, watch *how* I'm teaching you, so you can do that, too, one day."

Likewise, we're not born knowing how to use Word or Excel, or negotiate a complex deal that spans multiple nations and conflicting sets of laws, or devise a supply chain strategy so that all necessary ingredients and components are in place without wasting time, money, or space. We're not even born knowing how to safely get on and off the interstate. We have to be taught. Do we as children talk to the nice smiling strange man with the irresistible black Lab with the wagging tail? What did your parents tell you? What do you, in turn, tell your children?

Throughout the world, at every second of the day, there is evidence of someone having been taught something by someone else whose job, even sacred duty, it was to pass on the information. How to cook an egg. How to clean a fish. How to back up a car using only the mirrors. Righty tighty, lefty loosey. How to tie shoelaces. How to negotiate a better salary. How to navigate an emotionally charged conversation. How to sign up. How to beg off. How to pick a watermelon. How to pick a mortgage. How to build a factory. How to shake a hand.

For every tribal culture you belong to (workplace, community, club, religious), there are dos, don'ts, and this-is-how-it's-dones. Tribes depend on elders who are committed to patiently teaching the ways, hacks, tricks, timings, stealth, and dance moves to ensure the success, not only of the individual, but also the entire community of earnest, well-intentioned, eager-to-learn tribe members who only need to be shown how.

Values

Every tribe has values, whether they are intentionally and specifically articulated or not. Our values are what unite us; they bring us together in a protective ecosystem of our day-to-day work and decisions. Values also set us free. They are the guidelines that, once learned and embraced, release us to focus on the activities that make us successful—both as a tribe and as individuals. When clearly written, they tell us what our tribe cherishes above everything else. And what we should cherish first, then second, then third.

At WD-40 Company, the first value that supersedes all the others is, "We value doing the right thing." Because people will inevitably interpret "we value doing the right thing" differently, particularly if they are in multiple national cultures, we needed to define it more fully. And so, the following paragraph, published on the company's website, expands on the core principle:

> We do the right thing in serving our tribe, our stockholders, our customers, our products, our end users, our suppliers, and even our competitors. This means looking for the right action in every context and asking critical questions that bring out the best course or decisions relevant to the situation and the circumstances. It also means being honest in both word and deed. Being reliable, dependable and competent. And doing what's right according to the situation and the context. If we are honest and we speak and act congruently, we will be doing what is right.

Our values make our tribal culture come alive in the clear, unambiguous way they tell us all how we are expected to behave and establish our priorities. A strong values set also diminishes what we call "churn," that waste of precious resources, by repeatedly asking and answering the same set of questions, starting with, "What am I supposed to do now?" In an indigenous Australian society of centuries ago, values were more than a nice-to-have. They saved calories, which are crucial to survival. Living in a subsistence condition, there was nothing to be wasted on unnecessary actions or "noise" of life, such as these kinds of questions: "What am I going to do about this?

What should I do about that? What will happen to me in this gray area?"

Without values that supported the decision-making process centuries ago, those kinds of questions took up critical calories in the indigenous Australian society. Likely even causing someone to be killed by a wild animal or in battle. Today, values save time and money in the corporate setting. Well-articulated values eliminate fear-based second-guessing. They focus the tribe members' attention on what is most crucial. Whatever Learning Moment might result from the choices our tribe members make at any given point, if they make their choices based on our values, they're safe from retribution. They will be backed up by leadership. Whatever the outcome, that choice will become a Learning Moment. And the tribe confidently moves one more day into the future.

Belonging

My decision to include belonging as a tribal attribute came from Maslow's Hierarchy of Needs, in which after basic survival needs are met, belonging is the next crucial individual need. In the workplace, most people don't have—or don't want to talk about—their need for love and connection with their tribe members. The two questions people ask about in life are "Do I belong?" and "Do I matter?" Naturally, this entire conversation around the tribal culture is about belonging. Belonging is about creating an environment where employees can focus on building a future for their company because they aren't obsessing about their security and survival. They feel protected, supported, and safe to be authentic in both their personalities and the way they perform their work. And they feel accepted by their fellow tribe members.

Remember that your tribe members are there by choice. They can leave any time. You may have chosen them, but every day they choose to remain tribe members. This is where corporate leaders make a big mistake. The assumption is that once you have put the tribal culture in place, you can turn your attention away from your tribe and focus your energies, values, and priorities elsewhere. And soon you might find yourself to be the leader of a tribe of one—yourself. On the other hand, if leaders actually show their people that they care about them and that they belong, those tribe members will return the commitment in kind.

Future Focus

One of the key responsibilities of all tribal leaders is to create an enduring organization or group that can survive over time. Leaders need a future focus or they run out of options quickly. For instance, if you were a tribal leader in an indigenous Australian society that lived by a lake, it would be your responsibility to foresee a future where that lake might be dried up. So, even in those early years of plenty, you would still have on your mind the question, "How do we transport our tribe to a new lake so that there would always be water to sustain us?" It's that simple. Great tribes do this.

In a business setting, we are always looking at trends pointing to a variety of versions of the future. We must pay attention to the changing landscapes and architectures of the businesses around us. We must always be open to new ideas. That's where we will find the insights and innovations that will position us to thrive in an as-yet unpredicted environment.

We understand that where we are today is indeed a great place.

And we're comfortable being there. But we may not be here tomorrow. We may have to move to a new place to ensure that there is an abundance of what we need to be able to take us to the next new place in the future.

Future focus is also being mindful that no matter how detailed your visioning might be, many adjustments will have to be made as the reality of the future sets in. You can't do this alone. You must draw in talent—even unexpected talent with specialized skills—to help position your company to anticipate a variety of futures and be prepared to meet a new set of opportunities.

Leaders must look as far ahead as their imagination can muster. Ten years. Twenty. Why not fifty? Look ahead as far as you want your tribe to exist.

Specialized Skills

As I said, you can't do any of this alone. You must involve other people. My Fijian tribe leader reminded me that there are always people who are better than we are in doing what they do. In any tribe there are better hunters, better fishers, better builders, better spear makers, better fighters, better farmers. The job of the tribal leader is to know who is who, so they can be deployed exactly as they are needed, when their services are required.

It's not enough to know what is needed today—great leaders know what skills are likely to be needed around future corners, and who is most likely to be able to meet those demands. And then the planning and nurturing begin. In the corporate world, we talk about succession planning. Among tribes they talk about the future.

If, as a tribal leader, you don't have your radar tuned to discover what competencies might be needed, and how those competencies will help strengthen the tribe and the business, the tribe will start to weaken because other tribes now have the advantage. If you ignore the earliest signs of potential trends, you will be vanquished by your competitors.

Warriors

Business can be as fun as you want to make it. (Personally, I prefer a workplace culture where my tribe members are joyful in the work they do and who they do it with.) But let's not lose sight of the fact that it's also a competition, with serious stakes involved. To be a market leader, we must have a warrior spirit. We can be happy warriors, true. But we have to be warriors all the same. We have to be warriors for the cause of the company. But also for the sake of our fellow tribe members.

We need a collective understanding that all-out group effort in the service of a single mission is required. But it doesn't have to be grim and gritty. The spirit of tribal warriors can be uplifting and engaging.

In the corporate setting, the culture of happy warrior infuses the workplace experience with that unmistakable sense of "whatever it takes" commitment to the mission, even head-to-head competition with another company. There's a fighting spirit, to be sure, but there is also a sense of joyfulness, of play, of loving the game.

In modern-day tribes, the playing field could involve another business competitor. Or maybe it's last year's metrics you're trying to beat. Or maybe how well you create positive, lasting memories for your customers. Your field is our values, and you play to the expectations your tribal culture sets for you, as individuals and teams.

Celebration

In tribal cultures, members set time aside to mark important occasions and/or recognize star players. There is ritual of some sort, designed to call attention to the truly momentous moment. Warriors coming home victorious from a battle. Rites of passage for the youngest tribe members. Naming ceremonies. Noting the passing of a significant season. Appreciating a critical gift of time or even nature, like the rain or harvest.

At WD-40 Company, our earliest celebrations focused on product-related achievements. But our new tribal culture eventually shifted the focus to the people. As Ken Blanchard would say, "It's a shame that most people only know that they have done a good job because no one yelled at them that day."

Celebration is more than just a party. There might not even be a party at all. It might be just a cup of coffee and a piece of walnut bread in the break area. It was a mindset that took some time to take hold. But we would eventually celebrate a corporate anniversary. Or the smallest achievement. Even a Learning Moment that didn't quite work out as hoped. Above everything, it is the tribal leader's officially sponsored moment of appreciation—authentic, relevant, joyful, memorable, and reflecting all the tribe values in a single experience. Tribal celebrations must be culture-specific, aligned with the qualities you want to encourage, and memorable. Take time to celebrate. Don't celebrate the thing, but celebrate the people who gave the thing their all.

———

Assembling these seven components will turn strangers into friends, into respected and trusted colleagues, into cherished tribe members.

Or, on a less momentous afternoon, it will turn the chance sidewalk encounter into the beginnings of a friendship with a future that could turn out to be epic and life-changing.

By our shared tribal experiences and adventures, we shall know each other. And we will belong. And we will matter.

BEST: Get in the habit of thinking of your workplace environment as a community of tribe members, gathered together in a shared purpose and an inspiring vision of the future.

WORST: Insist on viewing your workplace culture as being made up only of individuals with siloed responsibilities, resumes, and self-interests.

FIRST: Consider all the ways your workplace is already a tribe in your traditions and the ways everyone interacts with each other. Build on what's already in place, using the seven components as a guide.

Chapter 3

THE BUSINESS CASE
FOR LEARNING MOMENTS

You've probably heard this story, but I bet some of your young-est tribe members haven't. Yet. Here's your chance to pass on one of those perspective-shifting leadership lessons that have helped hundreds of thousands of seasoned leaders around the world seed wisdom into the future.

It's a story that has been passed down through decades of young leaders. Even though it's not easy to nail down the exact details and accuracy of the original story, I still have faith in the essential truth of it. Here's how I remember it as it was told to me . . .

In IBM's earliest days, an employee made a very expensive mistake. The version I know has that mistake valued at $600,000. Naturally, when the mistake was discovered, the employee was fully prepared to be sacked. But IBM founder Thomas Watson saw the situation differently.

"I just spent $600,000 educating the man," he said. "Why should another company benefit from that investment?"

This is a tale of multiple Learning Moments. The hard knock the employee himself suffered was one, of course. But here's where the most valuable Learning Moment comes into play, over and over and over again through the decades: Every time that story is shared, new leaders learn that a mistake—however devastating to the company it might be—is a thing of value. Assuming, of course, it gets shared with others. That's how tribes learn not to do it again—through the free passing along of hard-won wisdom.

This story illustrates my favorite component of my leadership philosophy, the Learning Moment, which I have come to define this way:

> The Learning Moment is a positive or negative outcome of any situation that needs to be openly and freely shared to benefit all people.

What is the essential environmental ingredient that allows for the free and open sharing of Learning Moments? The reassurance that Learning Moments will not be punished. Amy Edmondson, the Novartis Professor of Leadership and Management at the Harvard Business School, refers to this environmental characteristic as *psychological safety*. I call it the *absence of fear*.

Recall the last half of the Dalai Lama's piece of advice around our purpose in life: ". . . at least don't hurt them." I can't think of anything more damaging to the human spirit (and the long-term prospects of a company that depends on bringing innovation to the market) than forcing our tribe members to do their best in a fear-based environment. Today's innovation-based organizations must be places where people feel safe to try new ideas and learn from the experience. But more often than not, the very human fear of potential failure strangles the learning spirit. The potential sting of shame and/or punishment that goes along with the disappointment of falling short of a reach keeps people from boldly taking themselves and the companies they work for into the future.

How do we remove that fear of failure? By redefining failure as an opportunity to benefit the entire tribe by the learning that results from that experience.

Behold . . . the Learning Moment.

I started developing my ideas around the Learning Moment around 1999 when I had the aha moment that caused me to ask myself, "Why are we calling these experiences *failures*?" They are actually steps on the way to a successful outcome. Sports fans know, for instance, that the best baseball batters on the planet have to endure hundreds of misses in order to achieve the batting average of .300. Thomas Edison famously referred to his thousands of attempts at perfecting the light bulb this way: "I have not failed. I have found 1,000 ways not to make a light bulb."

Don't we each deserve the same kind of grace in the workplace?

Even the name WD-40 pays homage to 39 attempts to achieve the formula that met our standards. Some would say those 39 episodes were failures. But each attempt brought us a step closer to the perfected formula. With each attempt, we learned something. Therefore, each attempt was a Learning Moment.

Okay, so I had developed the distinction. The next step was to insert it into our culture, which would necessitate convincing a lot of people that from now on it would be acceptable to fall short of a desired outcome in their sincere attempts at progress and innovation. This wasn't something that could be achieved in a memo announcing, "You can trust us. Really." Building this kind of trust would take time and experience, which, in itself, would be a Learning Moment for all of us.

I announced a new, fun challenge to everyone in the company: "We're going to have a yearlong program here, and I want you to share with me every month what your Learning Moments are. We'll have monthly prizes. And at the end of this year, the grand prize will be a round-the-world business-class trip with your spouse to visit our offices."

Naturally, it was a slow start. I didn't get many emails in the first couple of months as people slowly began to build up their trust in the process. I needed to prove to everyone that, yes, this is a safe place to take this kind of risk. So, periodically, I would announce and celebrate some of the emails I would get. I'd make heroes out of the first adopters, getting the word out about what some of the submissions were and what we were learning from them.

It took time to embed this confidence in our promise into the culture, so that they would be rewarded for being open, honest, and, most of all, sharing their experiences so that everyone would be able to learn from them. Slowly but surely, month over month, the pace of submissions picked up. People saw that this was a safe project for them. By the time the year was over, I was receiving over 100 submissions each month.

This was a numbers exercise. Because embedding trust in the Learning Moment concept as a supported value in the company was the most important objective, we didn't judge the winner by any perceived idea of what the merit of the Learning Moment was.

As promised, each month there would be a drawing. Consequently, participants improved their chance to win by the number of separate submissions they sent. And the year-end drawing was pulled from the collection of monthly winners.

As fun as the yearlong promotion was, it was most gratifying to see how quickly the idea of the Learning Moment was adopted by all the tribe members. And I could hear it in the halls, in meetings, in formal presentations, in passing: "I had a Learning Moment about this . . ."

No longer would we feel the need to hide our mistakes. This was a newfound freedom to feel safe in sharing them—not in the sense of confession but in the spirit of helping everyone learn from one another's experiences, the positive ones as well as the negative ones. As they started sharing Learning Moments with each other, they were actually taking action with the newfound knowledge. I began to hear more and more, "We learned that. We should try this instead."

Our Learning Moments soon become our knowledge base, one we *openly and freely shared to benefit all people.* Three thousand miles east of San Diego, at Harvard, Professor Edmondson was simultaneously developing the concept of *psychological safety* in the workplace—the experience so essential for confidently expanding the frontiers of original, innovative thinking, and then sharing the results with their colleagues. Without fear of shame or reprisal. Then they can focus on their performance, secure in the knowledge that their community of colleagues wishes them the very best and that the feeling is reciprocated.

Psychological safety is a concept first introduced in 1965 by the organizational culture pioneer Edgar Schein. And Edmondson has subsequently developed this concept to encompass the entire team experience, shifting the focus from production (which she calls "organizing to execute") to a "new way of working that supports collaboration, innovation, and organizational learning."

She writes in her book *Teaming: How Organizations Learn, Innovate, and Compete in the Knowledge Economy*: "Learning in today's organizations involves what's called *reciprocal interdependence*, where back-and-forth communications are essential to getting the work done." She goes on to describe the characteristics of an enterprise where a psychologically safe culture is essential:

- When the work requires people to juggle multiple objectives with minimal oversight.
- When people must be able to shift from one situation to another while maintaining high levels of communication and tight coordination.
- When it is helpful to integrate perspectives from different disciplines.
- When collaborating across dispersed locations.
- When preplanned coordination is impossible or unrealistic due to the changing nature of the work.
- When complex information must be processed, synthesized, and put to good use quickly.

Know any companies like that? Maybe yours? What culture in today's global business environment does *not* have any of these elements that require team members to work together freely, generously, and fearlessly? For this kind of culture to truly take root and flourish on its own, our people need to feel safe to bring new ideas and experiences to the table without fear of the possibility of punishment. Edmondson has called leaders' attention to the need for companies to emphasize their value on learning without reprisal as a key component to the psychologically safe culture. She writes in *Teaming*:

> This calls for workers who know how to experiment, how to think
> on their feet, how to work in the absence of rules, and how to
> adapt quickly. Knowledge, changing quickly within disciplines,
> becomes even messier and more uncertain when integrated across

disciplines . . . to get things done in the new workplace. Creating an appropriate environment for teaming and learning requires different management skills and expectations from those required in a repetitive task environment . . . today's managers need employees to be problem solvers and experimenters, not mere conformers.

Does the Learning Moment concept leave a company open and vulnerable to stupidity, thoughtlessness, and avoidable (not to mention very expensive) errors? It doesn't have to necessarily, as long as everyone understands what *acceptable failures* would be. As the years have passed, both Edmondson and I have been challenged by our respective communities to further refine our ideas about what an acceptable failure is, as opposed to just plain stupid or reckless behavior that threatens the health and well-being of both tribe and enterprise.

As you might expect, Edmondson's refinements are more nuanced than mine. In her 2023 book *Right Kind of Wrong: The Science of Failing Well*, she identifies three forms of failures that can occur in a workplace environment among thoughtful people of good intent:

1. **Intelligent failures:** She refers to these as "good failures," the kinds of disappointments "that are necessary for progress—the small and large discoveries that advance science, technology, and our lives."
2. **Basic failures:** She describes these as "the most easily understood and the most preventable. Caused by mistakes and slips, basic failures can be avoided with care and access to relevant knowledge."

3. **Complex failures:** Edmondson writes that these "are the real monsters that loom large in our work, lives, organizations, and societies. Complex failures have not one but multiple causes and often include a pinch of bad luck, too."

As for me, I share Edmondson's presumption of good intent. I rarely—if ever—came across a tribe member who intentionally took advantage of the Learning Moment concept to commit abject dunderheadedness or malevolence. In those cases, we would have been well out of Learning Moment territory anyway. Still, I have found that among two different kinds of sincerely authentic Learning Moments, as I have identified, one is more desirable than the other. I break them down this way:

- **More acceptable:** Those made in areas of experiment and learning.
- **Less acceptable:** Those made in areas of extreme demonstrated competence.

It's that simple. At least it can be. If we learn something new from experimenting, well, the company advances. If an experiment's likely result can already be predicted based on past results, a hard lesson already learned, or unvarnished common sense, we waste everyone's time and the company's money in an adventure that will most likely result in these words: "We could have told you so."

Is taking on the Learning Moments philosophy worth the effort and risk? Why not just stick to the tried-and-true and hope the company makes it to the next fiscal year with satisfied shareholders and inspired tribe members? Again, Edmondson says it better than I could in her *Right Kind of Wrong*, so I'll leave it to her:

Successful innovation is only possible as a result of insights from incremental losses along the way . . . Psychological safety helps people take the interpersonal risks that are necessary for achieving excellence in a fast-changing, interdependent world. When people work in psychologically safe contexts, they know that questions are appreciated, ideas are welcome, and errors and failures are discussable . . . [Failing well] allows people to ask for help when they're in over their heads, which helps eliminate preventable failures. It helps them report—and hence catch and correct—errors to avoid worse outcomes, and it makes it possible to experiment in thoughtful ways to generate new discoveries.

BEST: Expand the way you think about your company's story from more than simply objectives achieved quarter over quarter and year over year. Include the longer, heroic, epic narrative of all the brave and creative attempts of dedicated and well-intentioned tribe members who took big risks and then supported each other afterward, whatever the outcome may have been.

WORST: Punish your people for volunteering their Learning Moments. It only takes one violation of trust to destroy their confidence in the philosophy.

FIRST: Make your own Learning Moments public, no matter how embarrassing they might be. Your people need to see you out on that proverbial limb alongside them as everyone takes the initial risky steps together.

Chapter 4

YOUR PURPOSE IS NOT YOUR PRODUCT

Adults who grew up in the United States during the last decades of the twentieth century are likely to remember this ditty from *Schoolhouse Rock!*: "Conjunction Junction, what's your function?" The program writers were tasked to find an engaging way to teach a boring subject: grammar. So they came up with clever rhymes, a fun cartoon train station, and a new word for the kiddies: *function*. For millions of TV-watching children, it dawned on them that things were more than just things. They had purpose. "What's your function?" is just a fancy way of asking, "What are you for?" "What's your purpose?" Which is, actually, a more complicated, multilayered question than it might appear to be on the surface.

Starting from a child's point of view, for example, let's consider that box on the kitchen counter with slots in it. Eventually, as the child builds vocabulary, it becomes known as *the toaster*. Okay, great. But what's its function? Well, to toast bread. And then the questions begin:

"But why?"

"Because toasted bread is tasty."

"But why?"

"Because the crusty surface creates a solid foundation for adding warmed butter and the grape jelly that you like so much. And it gives me pleasure to serve it to you that way."

"But why?"

"Because it sends you off to school feeling loved. This is my way of telling you that you matter and you belong to our family."

Ah. There it is. A toaster, as it turns out, is more than just an electric box with slots and wires. It's a *love experience delivery system*. That's its function. To regularly and reliably make the recipient of said toast feel loved and valued. As another American commercial from that same era would remind us, "Nothing says lovin' like something from the oven."

And then we all grow up. The question persists, both personally and organizationally. What's our function? What's our purpose?

At the risk of sounding like a sap, I think that it's safe to say that we're all in the love experience delivery business. It's just a question of which niche we choose to be in. And exactly what experience we choose to deliver. But first, we have to get away from attachment to the product itself. And start looking beyond that item on the shelf to the human benefit, experience, or emotional transformation it promises. That is where we will finally identify and define our purpose.

When I first landed at my role at WD-40 Company, our purpose statement was still very much focused on the product on the shelf. We were fond of saying, "WD-40 is a great problem solver." And that made sense, given the utilitarian nature of the Multi-Use Product. Even today, the gallon can lists all functional deliverables: "Stops squeaks; removes and protects [exactly what it removes and/

or protects isn't made clear]; loosens rusted parts; frees sticky mechanisms; drives out moisture." Incidentally, it also makes snakes slippery, which turns out to be a handy advantage in some parts of the world, when it comes down to python versus public transit. We actually know that for a fact, from the experience of one of our customers, a bus driver in Hong Kong.

The slogans we coined during that era were more commercial taglines than they were purpose statements. And, I have to admit, we had some fun with them. We summed up our entire product line this way: "We are in the squeak, smell, and dirt business." But we didn't stop there with the jokes.

One of our products was 2000 Flushes. So, naturally, we said, "We're Number One in the Number Two Business."

That was us back then.

But soon, as I was to discover in my University of San Diego master's class with Ken Blanchard, I learned that there was much more to a company's purpose than simply the promise of eliminating that annoying squeak in a door hinge. Or that random smell coming from down the hall somewhere. (As I'm writing this, I'm now wondering if maybe there might be demand for a product out there somewhere that we can name Don't Blame the Dog.)

In Ken's classes on values and purpose, he helped me come to fully understand that a company's purpose is about more than what the product can do for the customer. It is about more than just the brand; it needs to be emotionally linked to the people and the world we live in. For WD-40, this included our tribe members. It had to make our people feel valued in the context of the work they do. I didn't think that being in the squeak, smell, and dirt business was something that our people would happily mention when a new acquaintance asks, "What do you do?"

"I'm in the squeak, smell, and dirt business" is not a response that encourages uplifting, happy conversation.

I was learning from Ken that a company purpose is one so compelling company-wide that it's embraced by everyone, head *and* heart, and acts as a unifying force. To be a great purpose, it would have people inspired to advocate for what they do, the people they do it with, and the people they do it for. It would provide a sense of stability and direction for everybody during periods of change or uncertainty. It would not budge, or waver, in other words, depending on circumstances, however extreme they might become.

So then I began to think about how we described WD-40 Company, and I knew it was time for a change. As I mulled it over for some months, I kept returning to the thought that people would say, "Oh, I remember a time when," whenever I told them that I worked for WD-40 Company.

As I reviewed those instances in my mind, I realized they weren't telling me about how well the product worked for them. They were telling me about the memory they cherished around the experience when the product was working for them. The squeak would be long forgotten. The circumstance around the removal of that squeak was the thing remembered lovingly. The time spent with a parent. Or a child. Or the time when a door hinge threatened to blow the whistle on a date that lasted later into the night than it should. And how the handy blue and yellow can with the little red top would play a role in rebuilding grandpa's tractor on the family farm that decades before you had had your first driver's lesson on. Or the time it saved the day on a long bicycle trip. Or a day out on the water, sailing. Or how it revived a critical piece of machinery that gummed up an entire assembly line, ultimately allowing the factory to make quota that day.

As it turns out, WD-40 Company figures into thousands of

positive, lasting memories throughout the world. That's its true purpose.

We are in the memories business. We're here to create positive, lasting memories with the customers we serve, the people in our tribe, the community that we're given permission to operate in. We would ultimately capture this vision in our formal purpose statement:

> We exist to create positive, lasting memories in everything we do. We solve problems. We make things work smoothly. We create opportunities.

During this time, we were also working on creating our values. And we said, "If we could align one of our values to what our purpose is, that would really embed it." Our first value became, "We value doing the right thing." And our second value became, "We value creating positive, lasting memories in all of our relationships."

Was this idea universally embraced right off the bat? Absolutely not. It was derided as being too, let's see if I remember the expression correctly, *foo-foo*. Just another softheaded notion from that crazy young Aussie who still had so much to learn about how things are done in American business.

I remember once when an advertising agency was pitching different brand positioning strategies. And I happened to be in that meeting. I said, "No, no, no, no. We're in the memories business."

And they laughed at me.

So I said, "I want you to think about it. What does a memory do? Firstly, it's created from an event. Secondly, it puts a stake in the ground of something that you can cherish or sometimes memories you don't cherish, right? The bad memories, we don't want those. But they are also something that we can talk about."

There was the predictable eye rolling, of course. But my voice was loud and emphatic enough that the agency team had no choice but to consider my point of view. So they packed up their laptops and presentation materials and marched off to consult the Oracle of Madison Avenue, or their Magic 8 Ball, or whatever it is that they do to confirm or concede their creativity.

In due time they came back to solemnly pronounce, "We're quite intrigued."

The result was the following wording: "We exist to create positive, lasting memories by solving problems in factories, workshops, and homes around the world. We solve problems, and we create opportunities." Yes, we kept the language around solving problems. A problem solved is also a positive, lasting memory, right?

"Creating positive, lasting memories" became the true north that governed every decision we made from that point forward. Including a critical decision to step up to the opportunity to create a product to go head-to-head with one of our most compelling competitors. Our challenge was to develop a penetrant that worked better than the competitor's did. The added challenge was that it would have no cancer-causing ingredients in it, as the competitor's did.

Recall that our number one value is *to do the right thing*. So bringing a known cancer-causing ingredient to the marketplace was out of the question. Cancer had touched many of us at WD-40 Company. My own brother had died of cancer. We were prepared to cancel the entire endeavor if that was to be our only option. Cancer did not bring lasting, positive memories to humanity.

Happily, our R&D team took on the challenge. The result was a product that actually worked better than the competitor's. The development process took longer, to be sure. We were slower to market than our competitor was. But the memory of how we all pulled

together, stood by our values and our purpose, and made the necessary sacrifices to create the product we would be proud of was the
memory that would outlast the short-term frustration of the earliest
days of development.

Years after we had collected many experiences and products that
confirmed and solidified our purpose, tragedy struck the Blanchard
family. Their house burned to the ground, taking with the flames
every material possession of both value and sentiment.

Ken's wife, Margie, would say to me, "The only things that you
ever get to keep are the memories that you have. We lost everything
in that house, but we still have our memories."

BEST: When developing your company's purpose statement,
look beyond the promise as it's described on the product
labeling and consider how the successful use of the product
makes people feel.

WORST: Settle for the first purpose statement that comes
to mind. If the successful outcome can be described in a
quantifiable way, you haven't yet touched the heart of your
company's mission.

FIRST: Invite your customers and tribe members alike to tell
you what the company and its products mean to them personally. Collect stories and insights. Your purpose will be
found there.

Chapter 5

THE FOUR PILLARS OF A FRICTION-FREE CULTURE

I n the previous chapter, "Your Purpose Is Not Your Product," I make the point (successfully, I hope) that a company's product line is not the thing that attracts, inspires, and engages raving fans— neither customers nor tribe members. But it can provide the frame in which to paint the picture, or tell the story, of that happy outcome when your tribe and product engage with each other. Being in the *memories business* is much more compelling, wouldn't you say, than telling new acquaintances, "I sell oil in a can."

In the case of WD-40 Company, though, our product line actually inspired our philosophy that shaped our tribe members' experience of being associated with lubricant.

You want things to run smoothly in your workshop? Reach for the blue and yellow can with the little red top, WD-40 Multi-Use Product. It delivers a friction-free experience for you. No-brainer. You want relationships, projects, and objectives to run smoothly among people? Likewise: Eliminate the friction.

And for that purpose, you need a different sort of system. In the case of WD-40 Company's journey, I chose to build it around what I call the Four Pillars of a Fearless Tribe:

Care
Candor
Accountability
Responsibility

They're not very glamorous at first glance. But they're essential. Imagine, for a moment, the subbasement of a spectacular skyscraper. It's not so pretty down there, to be sure. It's mostly bland concrete, specially formulated and poured to take on the weight of all that is above—all those details and amenities selected to please, inspire, communicate, transform, enlighten, and ignite the imagination of all who interact with the building and its occupants.

You are unlikely to see any of that in the subbasement. What you do see are massive, unadorned pillars. Considering the accumulated weight of all that they hold up, there are surprisingly few. In fact, the fewer the pillars, the better the engineering.

As we engineered the WD-40 Company's cultural structure over time, we found that these four pillars supported the entire experience of what it means to do business within the company. Each pillar is critical.

CARE

Imagine the company environment where you and your people go to work every day. As a tribe you contribute to something bigger than yourself, you learn something new, you feel safe and protected by a compelling set of values, and you go home happy. That's what a *caring organization* is.

As I witnessed the concept of Care come alive at WD-40 Company, I saw our commitment to creating that caring organization flip all the levers that make life inside a healthy community a good, rewarding, fulfilling place to be. The caring culture is an environment where people are given the latitude to apply the principles of basic human kindness, gratitude for all that we have, the pursuit of justice, trust, transparency in our relationships throughout the organization, and the safe experience of honest conversation (which we will explore further in the next pillar, Candor).

Let's first explore what the caring organization is not: It's not Friday night gatherings where we all sing "Kumbaya." It's not about making decisions that have the least amount of negative impact on individual self-interests in the short term. The caring organization is not a hug, a flower, or a brownie to soothe hurt feelings. The caring organization is not about creating a narrative where the CEO feels good about having the reputation for being a caring leader, at the expense of longer-term objectives.

There will be tough decisions. The caring organization strikes a balance between being tough-minded and tenderhearted. It's unconditional love—to the extent appropriate in a business setting—combined with the commitment to doing what you need to do to keep people safe. The caring organization creates the environment that expects you to do what you must to execute on a rigorous business plan so that it endures over time. Caring also means that every tribe member has a responsibility to care about everybody else.

When I consider the fundamental elements of the caring organization, along with its most basic promise, the word *trust* comes to mind. It is the ultimate value proposition of the caring organization.

To break this concept down into actionable components, we draw from Cynthia Olmstead's Trust Model, as described in *Trust Works!*, the book she wrote with Ken Blanchard and Martha Lawrence. It follows the simple ABCD format:

A—Are you *able*? Are you competent?

B—Are you *believable*? Do your actions reflect your words?

C—Are you *connected*? Do you take time to be with people in a meaningful, emotionally authentic way?

D—Are you *dependable*? Do you do what you say you're going to do? Can people rely on you?

Trust is the fundamental experience of the caring community. When you have trust, you have a tribe who will trust that you have their best interests always at heart. They will follow you into high-risk, long-term territory where great business outcomes will be found.

CANDOR

The second element in Olmstead's Trust Model is B for *believable*. A culture where everyone is believable (not just the leaders) is one where everyone feels safe to speak their truth as they know it. This doesn't automatically presume that everyone will agree with each version of the stated truth. But without a culture of safety where everyone can be counted on to express themselves, the entire community will forfeit the enriching benefit of all points of view.

On the other hand, the result of restrained truth is a toxic stew of half-truths, misunderstandings, critical decisions made based on only partial information, fractured relationships, stifled passions, and, before long, the regrettable departure of your most cherished talent.

This pillar of Candor shows up in actual behaviors: no lying, no faking, no hiding—period. In organizations, I really believe most people don't intend to lie—they fake and hide because of fear. How this shows up to the leaders: they must always be prepared to be open and receptive to unpleasant information. How this shows up to the tribe as a whole: each tribe member feels safe to take the risk of speaking the truth. In fact, when this pillar is installed correctly, on a cultural level, each tribe member feels more at risk for *not* speaking up.

The safety is in the communication. This is the open avenue to delivering the best self that every tribe member has. Truth, told respectfully and with positive intent, creates safety. Which actually starts with speaking truth to the power closest to you. That would be yourself.

Most people don't consider themselves to be liars. But it's safe to say that many people will fake and/or hide when they feel they must protect their best self-interests. They fear reprisal.

Faking is simply not being true to yourself and your values. We've all heard "fake it until you make it." People think, *I'm just going to fake this because I'm afraid that people will see that I don't know something everyone else seems to know*—for the record, they could be faking as well. Or, *People will think less of me when they realize that I'm the only one in the room who has a completely different perspective on this matter.*

Hiding occurs when there is something they don't disclose because there is fear of failure; fear of some sort of negative reaction, either from the tribe or tribe leaders; or fear of being caught in having done the wrong thing—or the right thing wrong.

In the psychologically safe workplace, we all hold dear the principle that when we behave in good faith and with good intentions, there is nothing we could do that would cause us to hide. And the spirit of the Learning Moment, which, as we know, is such a crucial component of the psychologically safe workplace, is being true to ourselves and sharing our error with our tribe members. When we do this, we are bringing additional wisdom and knowledge to the group as a whole. If we hide our mistakes, we would be depriving our entire team of essential learning.

The essential value of the psychologically safe workplace is the promotion of flow by the absence of friction. A workplace culture devoid of trust is an experience filled with friction. Candor removes that lack of clarity, deletes the confusion, smooths the surfaces of engagement of the rough, splintery texture of emotional sticking points. And Candor sets the stage for the clear exchange of ideas. This is the pillar that promotes a high-performing workplace culture.

This isn't to say that candor-based conversations are easy. Some can be tough to initiate, some even tougher to be on the receiving end. Candor is not permission to be brutal in the name of being honest. Candor must be accompanied by caring. All tribe members—especially leaders—should take extra care to fill the emotional bank accounts of their colleagues with positivity and supportive relationship interactions. This way, when the time comes for a conversation that requires uncomfortable candor, the trust is already there. Even the toughest conversation will result in strengthened trust that will prevail over the momentary discomfort of disclosure and discussion.

ACCOUNTABILITY

Simon Sinek once said, "Accountability is hard. Blame is easy. One builds trust. The other destroys it." It seems that in these modern times, *accountability* is seen as a negative thing—an occasion to punish someone should that person fall short of the agreed-upon standard or goal. That person is in the hot seat, and now must *account* for their disappointing performance.

The friction-free tribal culture has a different relationship with the word *accountability*. It's a two-way street in which leaders and their direct reports equally hold ownership of the way they perform their duties and what outcomes their efforts lead to. For this reason, for example, the job of the leaders is to make sure their direct reports have everything they need to succeed in their jobs. And all our tribe members hold ownership of making sure they have what they need to succeed and lead the company to its fulfilled objectives.

Accountability, as a pillar, is a mutual discipline. The disciplined commitment to results itself is, in practice, a freedom of sorts. When the company is committed to promoting accountability in its tribe, the individuals who demonstrate accountability also hold permission to do whatever is necessary to meet that accountability.

WD-40 Company's Maniac Pledge is an example of this philosophy in action. Years ago, a direct report spent a great deal of time explaining to me why a goal was not accomplished within the agreed-upon time. The blame was placed on a lack of critical information required to take the necessary action. After hearing the tribe member out, I observed the simple truth out loud: "In the same amount of time it took you to explain to me why this commitment didn't happen, you could have acquired the information you needed to get the job done."

And at that moment the Maniac Pledge was born, named after Aussie golfer Greg Norman, who was known for his maniac spirit. It reads this way:

I am responsible for taking action, asking questions, getting answers, and making decisions. I won't wait for someone to tell me. If I need to know, I'm responsible for asking. I have no right to be offended that I didn't "get this sooner." If I'm doing something others should know about, I'm responsible for telling them.

This spells freedom—the freedom that WD-40 Company tribe members feel is necessary to get their job done and meet their obligations to their own direct reports, as well as to their direct supervisors. They don't have the victim's attitude. They face the facts, learn, and move to improve.

Accountability is manifested by the assurance that each tribe member holds in carrying through with their commitments. It is an understanding and expectation culturally that each one will own the desired outcome and all the steps required to achieve that outcome. For everyone throughout the organization chart who depends on us to help them be successful as well.

Accountability is individual achievement. But it's also learning that we are responsible for sharing with the rest of the tribe. And the community celebration when that outcome is realized.

It's fashionable to talk about "accountability partners" today. These are people we meet at the gym, on volunteer teams, or in work groups who we must rely upon on regularly for mutual support in accomplishing our goals. But, really, our first accountability partner is the face in the mirror. Are we, as individuals, at peace with our actions and choices? If we have a face-to-face conversation (with our own faces) about how well we honor integrity to ourselves, how will we hold up in the investigation? When things go right, look out the window to find all the other people who contributed. When something goes awry, look in the mirror first.

We are each our own supervisors. And we are each our own direct reports. Are we giving ourselves what we need to make sure we succeed and that we help our company succeed?

RESPONSIBILITY

Let's revisit the Maniac Pledge. You probably have noticed that each item of the Pledge is driven by the words, "I am responsible for . . ." *Responsible* appears three times in the Maniac Pledge. In Accountability, we speak of the outcome. In Responsibility, we speak of the *relationship* each tribe member has to the ideal behavior that generates the outcome.

Simply put, Responsibility is a turbocharged version of Accountability. As a tribe, now that we know what we're accountable for, it's our responsibility to make sure those desirable outcomes are actually realized. We each take personal ownership of the outcomes, and it's up to each of us to do whatever it takes to make it happen. Consequences (rewards and negative feedback in its variety of forms) are attached to the Responsibility pillar.

Responsibility is each tribe member's personal relationship to their role in realizing the ideal outcome. It demands that each tribe member respond with the answer "me" when the world poses the question, "Who is there to act?"

When it comes to psychological safety inside the workplace, when each tribe member is confident that everyone else shares responsibility in the company's success, the entire community feels safe to invest hearts, minds, talents, efforts, and risks in realizing the company vision that everyone agreed to. Everyone has their part and role. And everyone performs exactly as expected, because everyone shares the responsibility of a successful outcome.

I'm reminded of a strategy in rugby called the *blind pass*. In American football, even nonfans know how marvelous it is to watch as a quarterback throws a long pass into seemingly empty air but with every expectation that a team member is on his way and will be positioned in the right place to receive the ball when it ends its flight and drops into his hands. You don't have to be an expert football fan to be impressed by the skill, strength, accuracy, and teamwork of that play.

Well, in Australian rugby, that pass is basically performed backward—hence the name *blind pass*. The quarterback is running, but throws the ball backward, without being able to see whether there is going to be a team member likely to receive the ball. That is Responsibility in action because the quarterback is psychologically safe in trusting that the pass will be completed and the objective of the play will be accomplished. There will be no wasted time, motion, effort, faith, trust, or ambition because everyone holds the assumption that the ideal of Responsibility is equally shared among them all.

NOW YOU HAVE A FOUNDATION

These four pillars are your foundation, upon which you can build strong and enduringly positive relationships among people who rely on your leadership. If you are the CEO, you have the highest likelihood of being able to spread these pillars around the organization.

If you are not the CEO, you can still influence other leaders by your example. People will want to work for you. When you have openings, internal candidates will flock to apply. Your group will meet and exceed objectives more often. Your employees will be coveted by other departments. You'll have opportunities for personal growth daily, because you will be investing in your own growth by working diligently to build and preserve the pillars of a friction-free culture.

BEST: Decide how important having a friction-free culture is to you personally and how essential it is to achieving your organization's strategic goals.

WORST: Assume that interpersonal conflicts are momentary with no lasting negative impacts on the culture.

FIRST: Watch how people interact with each other and quietly assess the strength of each of these four pillars in your culture. Consider how much work must be done to shore up the pillars that need attention.

Chapter 6

VALUES SET PEOPLE FREE

If you attend any of my speeches, there will likely come a point when you will hear quacking from the stage. Unless we're at a Peabody Hotel and their famous ducks have escaped their rooftop roost, I assure you there will be no feathers involved. It's just me describing the typical experience of someone in an average organization under pressure to make an important decision. In most organizations, they won't be allowed to make that decision by themselves. That decision is likely to be one that involves either money or ego, or probably both. Despite whatever assurances there might be to the contrary, there will be others eager to weigh in. The quacking ducks. All noise, feathers, fuss, and bother. Everyone wants a piece of the action. Of the glory. Of the control. *Quack, quack, quack.*

The more money and/or ego at stake, the more ducks will insist on being involved, each one with an individual opinion or assertion. The more quacking that will ensue. All at once. Anyone living by a body of water or under a migratory path will tell you what a nerve-wracking racket ducks make. Very loud, very bossy, very quarrelsome, and, let's face it, very disruptive to anyone who really just wants to make the right decision in a timely manner. Without ruffling feathers.

Any opportunity to make an important decision gets, shall we say, quacked up the duck power chain until it finally reaches the Big Mallard. This creature, a wonder to behold in all its positional glory, is likely to be furthest from the point where the essential expertise lies. But from that lofty level, proclaims the ultimate quack, a decision is made and is then sent all the way down the quack chain to the individuals who could have made the best decision on the spot. Ages ago. All by themselves.

What is preserved and protected? Power. Positioning. Ego. Standard operating procedure.

What is sacrificed along the way? All those things necessary for a culture that promotes individual passionate commitment to the purpose that ignites innovation and personal, positive, lasting memories. Trust among everyone throughout the organization. Individual confidence. Precious time. Likely money. Great ideas that don't get expressed. Very likely the best possible decision.

For decades, the workplace efficiency experts have been trying to return the decision-making power to those who really have the expertise to make the right decision the right way. Right away. This ideal is usually called *the self-directing team*. And, in truth and despite earnest attempts over the years, a solid example of such a specimen that lasts over time is still a rare bird. However close you may have come in your own workplace, all you need to shatter that ideal scenario is a new Big Mallard to quack, "Right. We're not going to do it that way anymore."

What is needed is a cultural attribute that prevails over any change in leadership or shifting of fortune. I discovered that a robust set of values statements are the key to sustaining essential guardrails in helping to shape decisions, while releasing our people to make the best choices for the organization and tribe. A solid set of values statements is, from my experience, the insurance policy that secures a consistent sense of freedom among the entire community of colleagues to feel confident in the way they choose to perform for the business.

Granted, we've all seen those "values statements" that are so trite and shopworn that they're barely visible anymore. You know those buzzwords as well as I do: *integrity, customer-centric, teamwork, excellence, innovation* immediately come to mind as examples. You find them on many company walls, on login screens, in employee handbooks, tacked on break room bulletin boards. They have largely become useless over time as they simply blend into the background. Or even violated when a leader chooses an action or makes a decision that makes a mockery of everything the company says it stands for.

Here's what we did differently at WD-40 Company. About the same time we developed our *positive, lasting memories* purpose statement that has carried the company over decades and into the future, we decided to seriously define our values and infuse them into everything we did and the choices we made. This is when we discovered another essential distinction that shifted our culture in an enduring way. Our resulting values statements would resonate with authentic legitimacy and serve as our partner in decision-making. They unleashed our tribe members to confidently serve the interests of each other, the tribe, our customers, and the company.

Where our purpose statement reminded us *why* we were doing the work, our values statements told us *how* to do it. Not in a step-by-step recipe way, but in terms of keeping the spirit of what we were about regardless of how the conditions might shift around us.

In conditions of calm or uncertainty, our purpose statement was always our ship's bow, pointing the way to our destination. Likewise, our values statements were our ballast. They kept us stable, upright, moving forward. They informed us how to *be* what we needed to be in order to *do* what we needed to do.

After a leadership off-site using the work of leadership thought leader Jim Kouzes, coauthor of the book *The Leadership Challenge*, and many months of socializing the language with our tribe, we confidently arrived at these values statements:

- We value doing the right thing.
- We value creating positive, lasting memories in all our relationships.
- We value making it better than it is today.
- We value succeeding as a tribe while excelling as individuals.
- We value owning it and passionately acting on it.
- We value sustaining the WD-40 Company economy.

And yet something was still missing. These six values gave us the guardrails on what to do to create positive, lasting memories. But they opened up yet another question: *How do we ensure we're doing the right thing within each value?* Each one of these values was subject to individual interpretation. We needed to achieve even more granularity, while still providing each of our tribe members the latitude and freedom to breathe life into the values in how we chose to serve them in our day-to-day decisions.

Back to the drawing board. After much discussion, we determined that each of these values statements would be accompanied by a very short description of what it looked like in action. Not so short that there would still be room for unnecessary doubt. Not so long as to withhold autonomy from our tribe members and find ourselves unintentionally returning to the quack power chain.

So we arrived at the following statements:

We value doing the right thing. We do the right thing in serving our tribe, our stockholders, our customers, our products, our end users, our suppliers, and even our competitors. This means looking for the right action in every context, and asking critical questions that bring out the best course or decisions relevant to the situation and the circumstances. It also means being honest in both word and deed. Being reliable, dependable, and competent. And doing what's right according to the situation and the context. If we are honest and we speak and act congruently, we will be doing what is right.

We value creating positive, lasting memories in all our relationships. As a result of our interactions with our tribe and stakeholders, we all will feel better at the end of the interaction than we did when we began; we will leave with a positive memory of it. Our stockholders should be proud to say they own our stock. Our customers should consider us a part of their business success. End users should be glad they purchased our products, telling their friends about the quality and utility of our brands. Our company name and our many brands should become known as emblems of quality, performance, and value. Our tribe members should consider each other valued friends and colleagues who share work, struggles, successes, life, and laughter over the years. If we successfully live these values, the result will be a higher degree of mutual trust and respect.

We value making it better than it is today. We value continual improvement. We are a learning organization. We are responsible for our own development and helping others to learn, as well. We celebrate our successes, then move on to new heights of achievement. We solicit ideas and solutions from all, and consistently look for ways to progress. We are comfortable with self-criticism and receiving constructive feedback. We take the time to recognize others who do the same. We endeavor not to repeat mistakes. We value the development of our people in order to enhance their skills and to improve their career opportunities. There is a special moment that occurs right at the point in time where a person gains an insight or new knowledge because of a particularly positive or negative event. We are constantly on the lookout for these "Learning Moments," because they are the fuel for continual improvement.

We value succeeding as a tribe while excelling as individuals. We recognize that collective success comes first. Our organization is a global company with many different locations and tribe members spread far and wide. But everything we do is geared toward the success of the entire company. And within the company are smaller groups, whether they are functional departments or teams defined by geography. The same philosophy applies in these sub-teams. We believe the individual can't "win" at the expense of, or apart from, the tribe. But individual excellence is the means by which our organization succeeds. And "excellence" is defined as outstanding contribution to the whole. Our mantra is "one world, one company, one tribe."

We value owning it and passionately acting on it. We get our shoes dirty. We are relentless about understanding our business and our role in impacting it. We are passionate about our end users, customers, and markets, and how we can positively impact them. We act in ways that maintain our traditions while positioning us powerfully for the future. We consider carefully, act boldly, and course correct as needed.

We value sustaining the WD-40 Company economy. We realize creating and protecting economic value for our tribe and its stakeholders is a tremendous responsibility. We take seriously the fact that many families are dependent upon the actions we take. We recognize and accept this responsibility.

But we still weren't done yet. One more refinement step to go. It's not enough to simply have a set of values disconnected from each other, with no linkage or logical flow from one value to the next. So now our task was to arrange the values statements in a hierarchical order that would govern the way we filtered our decisions according to *essentialness*. It's not quite accurate to say *importance*. They're equally important.

It was a question of which value is addressed first, then second, then third, and so on. Picture a set of traditional Russian nesting dolls. (Google tells me they're called *matryoshka* dolls. See? We both learned something today.) There are eight dolls in differing sizes so that they all fit inside each other, assuming they're properly assembled. Assemble them out of order, and some are bound to be left out. Assemble them in the correct order, and it all makes sense. Each one is *essential* not only to the whole assembly but also to create an environment for the one preceding it and the one following it to fit just right.

The same can be said of the hierarchical structure of your values statements when making your decisions and weighing your options. When you establish your values hierarchy early on, you make the decision-making process easier on yourself and your tribe. And you're setting the stage for your tribe to make decisions independently with confidence and the expectation that even if the outcome doesn't come out quite right, you'll still stand by them. Because they followed your established values hierarchy.

Let your values set drive your decision-making process in a hierarchical framework, and you remove time- and energy-wasting friction in your corporate culture. And you will build trust among your tribe.

Let me show you what I mean. When I teach university business classes, I challenge students with a case study exercise that pits very valid values against each other. Given all the variables, what is the "right thing to do" for the business? For employees? For management?

After the students receive the case study, I divide them into three groups. Group A gets to tackle the problem any way they want to. Total freedom. Group B must address the case study governed by the set of company values. Otherwise, they're free to strive for the solution to the case study any way they choose. Group C can also do whatever they want, but they are constrained by not only the values but also the values as they are addressed in a hierarchical system.

Because this is my class, I get to decide what the values are and in what order. So, naturally, I give them the WD-40 Company values statements. I send them off into their three groups to figure out a solution to the case study. By the time their allotted 20 minutes are up, the first group (the one with all the freedom) comes up with only frustration and sometimes even anger at each other. The second group (the one with values but no hierarchical structure) spent their 20 minutes arguing over which values are most important to serve first.

The third group, however, always delivers its solution first, happy as a group with the conclusion they've come to and satisfied with the outcome. Even in those rare times when individuals don't get everything they believe to be best for the solution, they're satisfied with the way the problem is solved.

What does this repeatable experiment tell us? In an organization where your values aren't hierarchically arranged, you get wasted time, friction, and futility. You build dissent among your people, trust is destroyed, and people often take things personally. Hard feelings outlast the immediate project and threaten the possibility of healthy problem solving in the future. Subcultures defined by shared points of view begin to form. And these subcultures are like the antibodies that invade the petri dish of corporate culture to devour the good qualities.

Values—along with their hierarchical structure—are the constraints that free us to turn our attention, energies, and synergies to the activities that matter the most to all of us in the long run. They keep our culture secure and supported while we extend ourselves into unknown variables, territories, and innovations that will take us into a prosperous future. Some might consider them too binding to foster creativity, but I would like to put to you these four ways they free us to do our best work...

1. **Values free us from churn.** Churn stops the free-flowing exchange of information because people begin to prioritize protecting themselves and their careers over the concerns and priorities of their teams and the company as a whole. Your people spend their energies and creative capacity on their self-interest instead of pursuing a solid, unified direction as indicated by your organization.

2. **Values free us from regret.** Not every tough leadership decision turns out the way we want it to. That's just a fact of life. But if we are able to "show our work," so to speak, demonstrating how we made our decisions according to the hierarchical structure of the preestablished values set, we can confidently stand by our efforts and say that we did our best. And we will be believed.

3. **Values free us to attract the tribe members we want in our organization.** You can clearly articulate what is most important to your company and culture, and set up your values in such a way that your candidates can see how they will belong in your tribe.

4. **Values free us to attract the right customers.** Simon Sinek says, "People don't buy what you do, they buy why you do it. And what you do simply proves what you believe." Customers who align with your why become your partner in creating positive, lasting memories. In recent decades, we have come to appreciate the power of inviting our customers to engage with us on levels that are more emotionally evocative than simply choosing a can of oil. We belong to each other—company, tribe, customer. And the ground we stand on is enriched by our shared values and the stories we tell each other about how we express those values every day.

In a values-run company culture, the *pleasure in the job*, as Aristotle put it, comes when our tribe members come to work every day feeling happy to be there, trusting their fellow tribe members, knowing that they will be supported in all they do, inside a circle of safety. That safety comes in the knowledge that they have what they need to not only do the right thing, but to do it in the right order.

BEST: Understand that values work best when they are carefully arranged in a hierarchical order. And they must be accompanied by a full description of how they are expressed through actions.

WORST: Assume that values are all the same and any list will do, as long as they sound good.

FIRST: Decide to engage your entire tribe in the process of developing your brand statements and what order they are arranged in.

"OUR PURPOSE IN LIFE IS TO MAKE PEOPLE HAPPY ..."

Chapter 7

"EVEN THE QUEEN SITS DOWN TO PEE"

have the teacup still. Right here, where I can see it from where I sit at my desk. I'm looking at it now. It's a Noritake pattern, Mardi Gras, likely from the late 1960s or early 1970s. It would be right at home on the *Mad Men* set. Not exactly my taste. But it was hers. And that's what counts the most to me. When I lift it and feel its soft contours under my fingertips, I am brought closer to my mum, who drank tea at her same kitchen table in the same house for over 70 years. It was her morning routine through the pregnancies and births of all her children, including me. Somewhere along that period of time, she was excited by the acquisition of a new tea set. Now that cup is the only thing that remains.

And it was in her hand when she delivered to me the leadership lesson that set the tone for the rest of my career. It came out as a stern admonishment to not get too big for my britches. (In Australia we say, "Don't get too big for your boots.") But it landed on my heart with a different impact that actually brought enduring relief and reassurance.

It was 1999. I had just flown into Sydney from Los Angeles, where I had just completed a series of meetings with a number of large Wall Street investment organizations, all of whom were eager to learn more about the opportunities WD-40 Company had to offer them.

As I always did upon landing in Australia, I headed straight to my boyhood home in Five Dock. This was the home where my dad told me back in 1987 when I was considering my job offer with WD-40 Company, "You can't go wrong with that stuff, Son."

At the time of this particular visit in 1999, my father was already gone. And my mum presided over her once noisy, busy house, now alone, sitting at the faded plastic tablecloth, with her teacup as powerful as a scepter might be. She had time to think about the goings-on of her now-grown children. And, consequently, she had something to say to me that morning.

It started out like this:

"Welcome, Son. Want some tea?"

"No thanks, Mum. I had some coffee on the—"

Bam! A cup of tea appeared before me. Fixed precisely the way I have always liked it.

"How about some breakfast? Hungry?"

"Really, Mum. Thanks, but no. I ate on the plane and my stomach clock tells me it's—"

Bam! A plate appeared before me filled rim to rim with my favorite Australian breakfast—lamb's fry with onions, bacon, and gravy. Obediently, I lifted my fork and tucked in, not fully appreciating the fact that there would eventually come a day when I would give anything for that taste again.

After some opening pleasantries and news about the family and the neighbors, she got down to business. Which was mainly some slightly begrudging observations about how everyone was proud of my advancement at WD-40 Company. Yes, yes, well. And how Dad was right to give me the advice he did. He sure was, wasn't he? I was indeed very fortunate to pay attention to what he told me.

"Yes, Mum."

And then she went for the coup de grâce.

"But never forget, Son, even the queen sits down to pee."

Nodding silently and focusing on my plate, I wisely resisted the smirking urge to respond with, "Well, I don't." I got her message. And she was clearly in no mood for back talk from her youngest, whose cloth diapers were probably still being used to polish the formal, less frequently used, dining table in the next room.

Since she taught me not to talk with my mouth full, I managed to say, "Yes, Mum," before taking another bite of her delicious Aussie breakfast.

Other up-and-coming, newly minted corporate leaders might have bristled at the affrontery, even coming from their mother. If a gigantic promotion, with all the global corporate responsibility that goes along with it, isn't the occasion of a shift in gears of respectful treatment, even within the walls of one's childhood home, when *would* "due respect" actually occur?

In my case, never. Which is exactly as it should be. I never lost sight of the fact that my earliest days of very good fortune came as a result of being handed off one career step at a time from one caring mentor to the next. Starting, in fact, with my mum and dad. On paper, I wasn't anyone especially special. I didn't even have the basics, really, that most corporate professionals have on their resume as they begin to climb the career rungs.

Not even college. I liked business. I liked people. I had very little patience and aptitude for the solitary, sedentary activity of book study. I didn't advance my academic education after high school until 27 years later, when I sat in Ken Blanchard's class. By then, I was already the CEO. I've learned from others at every opportunity, absorbing the examples and lessons of their successful behaviors. And making the note to self, "Don't do that," when I watched hurtful leadership behaviors.

But I never lost sight of the fundamental fact that my mum knew: "I'm just a traveling salesman from Down Under." Over the years, that description was elevated only slightly to the introduction I gave to audiences—"Consciously incompetent, probably wrong, roughly right CEO." And now I'm the consciously incompetent, probably wrong, roughly right Chairman Emeritus of WD-40 Company.

I must have done enough things right along the way to keep the job my mum was begrudgingly proud of. And the successes that WD-40 Company has enjoyed with me at the stick have been covered by *Harvard Business Review*, the *New York Times*, CNBC, a respectable handful of books, and more podcasts than I've been able to count. Every now and then I'm asked what authors have made the biggest difference in my development and success. Ken Blanchard, of course. Simon Sinek, naturally. Marshall Goldsmith, obviously. Chester Elton and Brené Brown. Whitney Johnson, most assuredly. The Dalai Lama, as you already know. And whomever I'm reading or listening to, at that particular moment, on flights across various oceans.

But there's one more author who made a huge difference, who might surprise everyone, except perhaps my mum: Robert Fulghum, the author of *All I Really Need to Know I Learned in Kindergarten*. The simplicity of his message informed and inspired all my day-to-day, interaction-by-interaction choices. Boil away the overcomplicated, highly sophisticated leadership theory and you arrive at the same basic lesson:

It's almost impossible to go through life all alone. We need to find our support group ... When you go out into the world, hold hands and stick together. It's dangerous out there—lonely too. Everyone needs someone. Some assembly is always required.

My mum is gone now. She joined my father nine years ago. The house is sold. The kitchen table, most likely without its faded plastic tablecloth, has been passed on to another family, where a new generation of children sit and squirm and fight the urge to dash away from their open textbooks.

As for me, I start every San Diego morning in my home office. As to be expected, the full set of Noritake china is long gone. And so, sadly, as of this writing, is the queen herself. But I still have my mum's teacup.

And I'm still standing—with a community of cherished friends, colleagues, mentors, and tribe members I have come to know over 30-plus years. My secret? I never forgot where I came from, who I am, and who I have come to serve, no matter my title or role.

BEST: Hang on to your lifelong friends, who remember who you were long before you started building your career and public persona.

WORST: Believe your own press releases, book jacket flaps, and speaker introductions.

FIRST: Pick up the phone and call an old friend you haven't spoken with in over a "fill in the blank" time.

Chapter 8

YOUR DUMB-ASSERY IS YOUR SUPERPOWER

You've been to speeches and lectures delivered by CEOs, community business leaders, the captains of industry. They all start out the same way. Before the main event, an MC steps up to the podium and reads from notes.

"We are so grateful to be able to welcome Whozits to the stage as our guest this morning. Whozits is a graduate from the most impressive business school in the universe, after having first earned a dual bachelor's from Major Ivy League College summa cum laude at the age of eight, with a master's in seventeen languages. Whozits then single-handedly turned around three companies in Chapter 11 while captaining the yacht *I'm So Fabulous* to a victory in the first-ever longitudinal global race with a waddle of penguins for crew. Please welcome Whozits, who has so graciously agreed to step away from celebrating the new release of Whozits and the Gang's rock/country crossover album, hitting number one on the charts within the first nanosecond of dropping. Today we shall learn how to fashion a linear particle accelerator entirely from the paper straws left over from our last all-hands party."

Me? When I give speeches, I like to introduce myself to the audience this way:

"Hello, I'm Garry Ridge. I'm consciously incompetent, probably wrong, and roughly right."

Who would you rather sit next to at lunch? Okay, I get it, Whozits. Who wouldn't want to be enthralled by another 45 minutes of stories of derring-do? So let me rephrase.

Who would you rather work next to, year over year, in a collegial atmosphere of free exchange of ideas with a CEO who is open to mind-changing insights from the entire tribe?

I don't know about you but I choose the dumb-ass. I have found that those who embrace their own personal level of dumb-assery, and fly that flag high, are the most interesting ones to keep company with for the duration of a quarter, a season, a career. They're the ones with the best stories. And they'll give you a chance to get a word in edgewise. If you are like-minded, come sit by me. I'm eager to hear what you have to say.

Now let's switch roles. If given the choice, and a reasonably equipped IQ, who would *you* rather be in your own leadership role? A Whozits? Or an everyday bloke who works with people who can easily volunteer their opinions, insights, expertise, and, well, Learning Moments? If you've come this far in this book, I'm assuming you and I are cut from the same cloth. Come sit by me.

But there's a price to this kind of leadership style. You must come to terms with your inner dumb-ass. Your dumb-assery is your superpower, if you know how to use it.

I discovered the value of being the dumbest one in the room when I first landed in San Diego. This, for me, was the time that most of us just beginning a senior leadership role might feel the most pressure to send the impression that we're on top of all the things going on around us. We feel compelled to make our mark early with a rock-their-world opinion or a bit of knowledge. And when we have neither? We think to ourselves, *Well, I'll just listen, nod knowingly, and figure it out later when no one's looking. No matter what, I won't look stupid. I won't look stupid. I won't look stupid.*

In the early weeks of my arriving at my new job, a high-level senior leadership meeting had convened to hear the very sophisticated presentation of a much-respected outside consultant. He had some extremely important things to say to us about the direction of the company. But I was lost from Minute One. Have you ever had that dream where you're in a room full of people speaking incomprehensibly and you are the only one who isn't understanding a word of what is being said? It was like that. Only in real time, in real life.

I glanced around the room. Everyone was nodding in agreement and studiously taking notes. Giving in to the undeniable reality that I was completely lost, I put my pen down, sat back in my chair, and just watched the dynamics around the table. Could it really be that I was the only one in the room who was living out that nightmare? Well, I guess I was. Time to speak up and fess up.

"Sorry to jump in here," I began. "But I don't have a clue what you're talking about."

I expected to feel like the odd man out, clearly underqualified for this new position. Perhaps regretful that I had sold my house back in Australia. Instead, I was surprised to witness a subtle shift in pressure in the room as everyone let out of sigh of relief. *No one* knew what was going on! But no one had the nerve to admit it! (Between us: I would have put money on the likelihood that the consultant was in the dark as well. The words sounded good. The math added up. The charts and graphs were impressive. And everyone was nodding. So something must have been making sense. No? No. Oh.)

And then it dawned on me. As the new leader of a freshly developing culture (which was still just a hint of a glimmer in my mind as I was soaking up knowledge as fast as possible), it would be my responsibility to create a workplace where it would be safe for all of us to not know or understand everything before us from time to time. Which isn't to say that the tribe members wouldn't be responsible for finding out what we needed to know. But there would be no shame in the discovery of not knowing.

The first person who would have to admit, "I don't know," on a regular basis would have to be me. This wouldn't be an *abdication* of the responsibility to know things. It was a life philosophy that put the personal responsibility of being honest and humble squarely on all our shoulders. We were equally responsible for knowing—and understanding—those facts, strategies, and considerations put before us in our work. And consequently, we would be expected to own up to those times when we just didn't know something.

As for me? I had to lead the way in my own behaviors. How safe would your tribe members feel to admit they don't know something if you peacock around making sure all the world never forgets how smart you are?

This ultimately led to the Maniac Pledge, which we've already discussed, but I'll repeat here to refresh your memory:

> I am responsible for taking action, asking questions, getting answers, and making decisions. I won't wait for someone to tell me. If I need to know, I'm responsible for asking. I have no right to be offended that I didn't "get this sooner." If I'm doing

something others should know about, I'm responsible for telling them.

Simon Sinek, the author of *Start with Why*, says, "The risk you run is that sometimes you get humiliated. But not always. Sometimes you will get people who will say, 'Oh my gosh, me too.' But you worry that you are the idiot. If you let that stop you, you won't get the great answers."

What kinds of answer might you get if you ask the questions and let others do the talking?

You learn what the experts know. People feel good when they can hold the floor on the subjects they know best. We all tend to get expansive when we have a rapt audience. So let the experts expand. And expand our knowledge in the process.

You learn what your tribe members know and don't know. Let's say you're in a meeting with your tribe. Multiple levels are present. Throw out a question and sit back to watch what happens next. Likely your immediate direct reports will jump in and answer your question. You're their boss; they want to impress you. Your wise direct reports, however, will also sit back, stay quiet, and watch to see how *their* direct reports will answer the question.

And if you're sitting back, quietly observing who's doing the talking, you'll have the chance to observe which of your leaders are allowing their own dumb-assery to take the back seat and giving *their* people the chance to demonstrate their value.

Almost everyone who achieves a senior leadership role thinks they're supposed to have all the answers. But they have to remember that their job is now to lead others into developing, knowing, and sharing the answers from their unique points of view. If they are going to be true leaders, they have to model your behavior, and stay quiet to let others share what they know.

This means that, as with every other behavior in your organization's culture, accepting your own dumb-assery starts with you. It's likely to be one of the smartest things you do for your tribe.

BEST: Appreciate the fact that you are surrounded by people who likely know more than you do. Welcome the opportunities to have your mind changed every day.

WORST: Rely on bulleted lists of accomplishments on resumes as indicators of a person's ability to lead. Accomplishments don't tell the story of all the Learning Moments that occurred to achieve the objective.

FIRST: Get into the habit of saying, "I don't know," and asking, "What do you think?"

Chapter 9

THE WILL OF YOUR PEOPLE WILL MANIFEST YOUR VISION

D on't sell your house! You'll be back within five years and you'll want that fallback position!"

My mates meant well as I slowly let the word get out that my family and I would be moving from Australia to San Diego. I had just been offered the Director of International position at WD-40 Company, and I had accepted the assignment to transform it from a well-loved, highly recognized brand domestically (with growing but still modest European, Asian, and Canadian markets) into a global must-have in homes, factories, workshops, and offices all over the world.

Would the world embrace the blue and yellow can with the little red top? Did I have what it would take to transfer my belief in the WD-40 Company to consumers and distributors worldwide who had yet to even hear the brand's name? Would we be able to persuade millions of people in 176 countries to put back their go-to, tried-and-true lubricant and reach for ours instead?

There was only one way for me to find out. And that was to go all in. You may have heard the story about the man who made progress on his epic life's journey by "throwing his hat over the wall." By throwing his hat over every wall he encountered that threatened to block his progress, he had no choice but to scale that wall to retrieve it. And then carry on. (This story was a favorite among motivational speakers a while back. Now that I think about it in the context of these days, it sounds more like a story about trespassing. But you get the drift and spirit of the message. I hope. Moving on . . .)

By deciding to sell my house, I had thrown my hat over the proverbial wall. There would be no scurrying back to the safe, known territory I had called home for more than three decades. Where my friends and family were waiting for me to change my mind and come back home.

Little did I know that in just three years, the CEO at the time, Jerry Schlief, would announce his retirement and that the board would extend the offer to me to be the next CEO. Along with the assignment, *it had engaged my will.* It would be up to me to make something a reality that did not yet exist except in the minds of the board, Jerry, and maybe a few eyes-only, ultra-confidential strategy documents.

My job—and honor, really—was to manifest the vision. *To make it real.* Not only for the company's leadership but for everyone who would engage with the company, and its products, worldwide. There would be no turning back.

On my flight across the Pacific to San Diego, I thought about what I had going for me as I took on this new adventure. A product I passionately believed in. A company I was equally committed to.

The support of leadership who had faith in me. The earliest sketches of a strategy that only needed time and better minds than mine to help solidify. A thorough understanding of my own limitations, that's for sure.

And, more valuable than anything else, I had good friends throughout the entire company. Having already been working at WD-40 Company for eight years, my memory bank was a scrapbook full of scenes and stories of working together, traveling together, celebrating together, learning together, and teaching one another, and taking on each new challenge and competition like the happy warriors we were. There were anniversary parties, weddings, picnics, cake cuttings in the break room, funerals, moments when we dropped what we were doing to help out a mate who needed a hand. And there was that one time when I had led a busload of mates in a rousing rendition of "Tie Me Kangaroo Down, Sport" on a trip back to San Diego from Tijuana.

And I understood that *the will of the people* would be the magic formula for creating this dream and turning a vision into a reality. They were the ones who would breathe life into this idea that we had for ourselves.

I then returned my thoughts to the strategy we were developing to introduce the product itself around the world. Based on what we had learned while opening up new markets in Europe, Australia, Asia, and Canada, we knew that authentic connection depended on the affirmative answer to these three questions that made up our strategic framework:

- Do you need me?
- Do you know me?
- Can you buy me?

These three elements were critical to building brand and building consumer and user acceptance for many years. While we were wondering how we could amplify those elements to spread the WD-40 brand value proposition globally, we also began to explore ways these same questions could apply to the process of engaging the will of our people.

It wasn't a matter of building factories; it was a matter of creating a culture that we're going to spread all over the world. It was all about the individual's choice to engage with us, either as a customer or a member of our team (we hadn't yet developed the *tribe* concept at this point). How do we set a culture up that allows people to have a choice? We knew that as much as we couldn't force customers to buy our products, we also couldn't micromanage WD-40 Company employees into adopting the will to win. The answer, as I was soon to learn directly from Ken Blanchard himself, was to engage through *their hearts*.

This revelation was the beginning of a decades-long Learning Moment that I'm still on. But back then, in one of the first of his presentations I had the privilege of sitting in on, Ken said that most MBA programs get people in their head.

He said, "If we are really going to build sustainable organizations over time, we've got to start getting people in the heart as well. It's about the heart. This is how we build an organization where people go to work, do great work, and enjoy it. And, therefore, the work is better work.

"A positive corporate culture is the key to attracting and retaining top talent, driving innovation, and achieving business success. By prioritizing employee well-being, diversity, and inclusion, companies can create a workplace culture where everyone can thrive."

The challenge to me was not about strategy. The challenge to me was about creating the catalyst where we don't have to micromanage them into a fearful state to activate the strategy.

We would create the cultural environment that allowed people to have what they needed to actually succeed. Revisiting the three-part strategic framework, we soon learned that there were corollaries in the experience of employee engagement and culture.

- **Do you need me?** Do the employees crave a working environment where they belong to something that is purpose-driven and meaningful? Do they want a day-to-day feeling of connection, where they know that they matter and that they belong? Where they can work in the company of fellow employees who support, nourish, and protect each other?

- **Do you know me?** Does the WD-40 Company brand promise of creating positive, lasting memories resonate with their deepest emotional desires for meaningful work? Does their experience of the culture fulfill their yearning for purpose? (If, for instance, when WD-40 Company doesn't speak to that drive for purpose, it's just selling oil in a can. A pretty blue and yellow can with a jaunty red top. But a can, all the same. Who gets excited at their deepest heart level by oil?)

- **Can you buy me?** More to the point, in terms of a thriving culture of employee engagement, do you *want* to buy my opportunity to join our community? Do our mission, vision, strategic objectives, principles, values, and processes make sense to you in an accessible way? Can you see yourself building your own future in this community of true hearts working toward the same vision?

This is the will of the people. It's that spirit that encompasses morale, inspiration, commitment, and a desire to offer discretionary effort.

Inspired by our successful story of taking the blue and yellow can with the little red top all around the world, I came up with this formula that has since served us well:

The Will of the People × Strategy = Success

BEST: Believe that your people want to be "hat over the wall" invested in the success of your company's strategic vision for a transformed future. Resolve to be worthy of that commitment.

WORST: Assume high-level strategic planning is strictly the property of C-suite leaders.

FIRST: Include all your people as essential partners in co-creating the vision to make it real.

Chapter 10

CURIOSITY COLLECTS MORE CUSTOMERS

The typical innovator/entrepreneur journey usually starts in one of two ways.

The product idea comes first. It's such a great idea, everyone will love it! And they will immediately bring it into their lives. It's so great! The light bulb. The smartphone. The pet rock. The fidget spinner. The KitchenAid stand mixer. Doesn't matter. The benefits are instantly obvious. They'll fly off the shelves! Who can't see how this great new thing won't improve their lives in very obvious ways? It's a no-brainer!

Or the perceived unmet need comes first. What the world needs now is a better mousetrap. Or, let's just say for illustration's sake, a masterfully formulated lubricant. Sure, it will take 40 tries to get the formula just right. But once it's ready for market, boy oh boy, it's going to be in every kitchen, garage, and workshop around the globe. Who doesn't have at least one squeak in their life that needs dealing with? It's a no-brainer! (And for some extra eye-catching pizzazz, let's give it a jaunty red top.)

We have the unmet need. We have the product idea. Let's get down to work on manufacturing, packaging, marketing, promotion, and distribution. And then we sit back as the world is wowed by this great new thing we're bringing to the clamoring public. They may not know they want it now. But when they get a load of how wonderful it is, the early adopters will carry the word about us throughout the world. High cotton! Easier than falling off a log.

But what happens if our identified customer base has other ideas? And they just don't care about the solutions we provide to problems that don't exist in their world? Time for more questions. I learned that lesson firsthand one year at an auto trade show in Beijing.

Selling lubricant to the auto industry. With all those moving metal parts in their world, who wouldn't jump at the chance to employ our superior product in their operations? This was going to be a fun and exciting trip. My big challenge was to learn two new words in Mandarin Chinese: *yàngpǐn* (sample) and *rùnhuá* (lubricant).

There I stood at our WD-40 Company booth with little samples of WD-40. "*Yàngpǐn rùnhuá! Yàngpǐn rùnhuá!*" Here is a sample of lubricant! On my mind: *I hope we don't run out with all the demand that will be coming our way.*

But the Chinese conventioneers were just walking past me, not paying any attention.

My Chinese must be really bad, I thought. Naturally I double-checked with my Chinese buddies, those who I knew would be honest with me.

"You're saying it right," they reassured me.

"So why don't they need my WD-40?"

That was when I noticed another booth down the row where there was a long line as far as I could see. What were they giving away? Trade shows are full of cheap freebies that appeal to the inner child within us all: cookies, chocolate, little plastic toys. ("It's for my son when I get home," you volunteer, embarrassed that you would come all this way and stand in a line so long for a wind-up toy that is really for yourself.) So I thought, what are *these* guys giving away that's so great?

A small brown paper bag with a string handle on it. Even more baffling: an *empty* paper bag.

I returned to my Chinese mates and asked, "Why are people lining up to get a brown paper bag with a string handle on it and there's nothing in it?" I added mentally, *Yet they don't want my WD-40, which is going to be very useful for them. There's something not right here.*

The booth owners knew their customer. This particular brown paper bag was the perfect size for accommodating the perfect size scoop of rice that would go with their customers' lunch. It may have been empty now, but it would be exceedingly useful later. And the prospective customers could tell this at a glance. So, they lined up for one of their own. That booth knew what these people needed and wanted.

It was a matter of an unmet need, I reasoned, trying not to feel sorry for myself. They needed the convenient little bag. So they lined up for it. They didn't need this fantastic lubricant that I was offering for free? How could that possibly be? Especially in the auto industry? Was our plan for expanding WD-40 Company into China doomed?

This mystery called for more questions. So my booth buddies and I roamed the exhibit hall and asked people one simple question: "Why don't you need lubricant?" As it turned out, it wasn't an unmet need. Any time they needed to lubricate anything, they would just use the dirty diesel oil that was always plentiful in their shops.

And it was free. Why would they want to pay for something they already had more than enough of?

But rust was the issue for them. There was the unmet need. *Well, we can help with that.* So we changed our message. Same product. Different value promise. Different message.

"Here's a sample of anti-rust oil." (Needless to say, I asked for expert help on the translation into Mandarin.)

Within minutes we had a crowd to such an overwhelming extent that we needed to engage professional crowd control help. I could have walked away from China convinced that there would be no market for our oil. Instead, our whole marketing platform in China was established around the message that we were not just selling lubricant; we're selling an anti-rust oil. *Voilà.* An unexpected, undiscovered, unmet need. Now it's an opportunity.

All we had to do to convert the entire China auto industry was to simply ask a few more questions. And be willing to change our tune, attuned to what they needed, rather than what we wanted to give them.

If you stay curious, your customers will continuously surprise you with their own innovative approaches to using your product to make their lives better, easier, and friction free. So, over the years, we made a point of asking the question, "How do you use WD-40 Multi-Use Product?"

As we approached the turn of the millennium, while other companies were worried about Y2K implications on their computer systems, we were asking ourselves, "Do you think we can get as many as 2,000 responses if we ask our customers to tell us what they do with WD-40 Multi-Use Product?" We need not have worried. We received over 250,000 responses. It was a fun challenge to find 2,000 winners. Here are just a few from the published list:

- Lubricates seat belt buckles
- Removes gunk from ostrich eggs
- Buffs out scuff marks on car bumpers
- Helps to insert cables into cable looms
- Shines car tires
- Removes stubborn temporary tattoos
- Removes Play-Doh from hair
- Removes gunk when replacing old faucets
- Loosens rusted parts of an antique farm dinner bell
- Unsticks piano keys
- Removes crayon marks from walls
- Removes hair color dye from towels
- Removes tea stains from countertops
- Removes crusted gunk from birdcages
- Keeps rabbits and rodents out of gardens
- Shines seashells
- Removes tree sap from metal Christmas tree ornaments
- Shines doll shoes
- Keeps beard trimmers working well and quietly
- Removes dog poo from tennis shoes

And then there is the aforementioned fan favorite: removes a python from the undercarriage of Hong Kong public buses.*

One Reddit user once reported, "I used it 10 minutes ago, I feel like my life is now complete." I suppose it might have some existential applications. But those would definitely be considered off-label.

---

* For a complete list of the 2,000 uses, visit https://www.datocms-assets.com /10845/1562642906-wd402000usesupdatedjan2017.pdf. It's fun!

BEST: Assume that no matter how well you know your product, your customers know it even better in ways that would amaze you.

WORST: Stubbornly refuse to listen to fresh ideas, especially when they come from customers.

FIRST: Routinely ask, "What else can we do with this?"

Chapter 11

THE COACH'S BEST GAME IS OFF THE FIELD

He was a great guy who was having an absolutely terrible day. Something was really bothering him. Maybe problems at home? Maybe some kind of untenable frustration with a project in his business unit? I didn't know. But this normally affable tribe member, so collaborative, so creative, so relaxed and funny, had brought Opposite Man into a brainstorming meeting one afternoon. And everyone around the table shifted uneasily in their seats as he ranted, barked orders at the group, and interrupted the others before they even had the chance to complete a sentence. He dismissed proposed ideas before the speaker could complete a thought. The rest of the meeting participants gradually shut down. You could practically see their engines power down. One by one, one after the other. They all silently watched their cherished tribe member, well, lose it. Right there in front of them.

While other leaders might have jumped in to save the meeting—most likely escalating the tension and embarrassing everyone—I just sat back and watched. The time to talk with him was not right then and there. But that time would come during the much-needed break.

"Let's take a walk, Dave," I said. (Dave isn't his real name, of course. You understand why I don't use it here, I'm sure.)

"Sure," he said, looking at his watch, signaling that he'd rather do anything in the world than take a walk with me. Not in the mood he was in, that's for sure.

With that, we took a stroll around the campus. I started making a big show of looking for something. Behind park benches. Under cars. I peered around signage.

"*What* are you looking for?" he asked impatiently.

"Where is my very good mate Dave? I'm looking for him. The Dave I know and love was not in the room," I responded. "I saw him here just yesterday. You probably know him. That really nice guy, whom everyone loves to work with. The one always quick to offer a kind, encouraging word and to listen to others when they speak. He seems to have sent in an impostor to this meeting this morning. But he must be around here somewhere."

Dave got the message. He didn't need a dressing-down. He just needed to be reminded of who he was, how we all see him and value him on not just his best days but even on ordinary days. And he needed that support in the confidential setting of a one-on-one Learning Moment. Not in front of the entire room where in a different setting someone might have said in front of everyone, "Dave, you're being an ass. Shut up."

Dave didn't need to be told he was being an ass. He needed to be kindly walked back into the wonderful person he really was. He needed—and deserved—a coach who was more interested in helping him be his most excellent self. In private. Off the field, so to speak.

He also didn't need any more input from me. When we returned to the conference room, he started off by apologizing to the entire group for his behavior. The understanding tribe immediately forgave him and we returned to our business at hand. His dignity was preserved, and trust in the entire group was reinforced. And all I had to do was a little private performance coaching in the parking lot. With an audience of just one.

Back in 2005, we made the decision to stop using labels like "boss," "supervisor," "manager," or, the absolute worst of all, "superior." (Whoever wanted to be *superior* to anyone else inside WD-40 Company was definitely not a good fit for our culture.) No. We were *coaches* and we had coaches ourselves. We were a tribe of individuals thoroughly invested in the mission of helping each other do our very best work in the spirit of a team pulling together to win at work.

What's the difference in the two leadership philosophies?

The boss role implies the outdated, command-and-control job of *driving* a person's productivity (and, in a variety of escalating ways, punishing failure to perform). But a coach's role is to *inspire*, *nurture*, and, in all possible ways, *bring out* the person's unique level of excellence. The coach provides all the necessary support, training, and emotional encouragement to elicit performance that everyone can be proud of.

As we gained more experience in living out the concept of coach instead of boss, I came to realize that much of the leverage that a boss has comes in the form of performance reviews—both the formal annual review that almost everyone despises anyway and simply the day-to-day stress of judgment task by task, assignment by assignment. It's emotionally exhausting and depletes trust and confidence in the relationships among tribe members.

I started to develop this approach to leadership, which I

eventually would call "Don't Mark My Paper, Help Me Get an A." I discuss this approach in greater detail in the book *Helping People Win at Work*, which I wrote with Ken Blanchard in 2009. As coaches, our role is to help our tribe members succeed in real time, not stand back and grade the performance later. So it became obvious to me over time that when a tribe member's performance didn't meet potential or expectations, the problem was the coach's, not the tribe member's. Once that new distinction was ingrained in our culture, we determined that in those very rare incidents, it was *the coach* who needed further coaching.

We also took a page out of the coaches' playbooks in the sports world. Coaches do what they do best. Which means that they support their players in doing what *they* do best. Meaning: They stay off the field of play, providing support and guidance from the sidelines. Let's just say, no fullback on an Aussie rugby team wants to see his coach inserting himself directly into the game. While coaches know how to guide and nurture excellence, performance, and strategy in the game, they do it from the sidelines. And they know to let the players play instead. After all, the players are better equipped to deliver the results everyone wants.

Granted, there are celebrity coaches, just as there are celebrity CEOs. But when the game is in play, the stars of the show are the people doing all the action-oriented things necessary for the win. And the coaches know their place, which is well out of the way of the action.

Bosses deplete trust and confidence in their people. Coaches infuse trust and confidence in not only the individual player (or tribe member) but also the entire team (or tribe) culture. They achieve this through ongoing open-ended conversation, not top-down transfer of information (or threats) from boss to direct report. I think that

Michael Bungay Stanier's book *The Coaching Habit: Say Less, Ask More & Change the Way You Lead Forever* has to be my favorite book on this subject.

In this book, he offers an in-depth discussion about seven essential questions that coaches can employ to bring out the most powerful insights from their clients (or, in the case of a company culture environment, tribe members). Stanier lays out his seven questions in such a way that they combine to support the coach's primary assignment, which is to help the tribe member succeed. They are:

1. "What's on your mind?"
2. "And what else?"
3. "What's the real challenge here for you?"
4. "What do you want?"
5. "How can I help?"
6. "If you're saying *yes* to this, what are you saying *no* to?"
7. "What was most useful for you?"

Notice that his questions do not include the word *why*. *Why* stops the play, and demands that tribe members defend their actions. When coaches ask *what*, they are asking their tribe members to teach *them* what they need to get that proverbial, most desirable A. It's a partnership of cocreation. Safely done well outside the actual field of play.

These seven questions starting with *what* create a safe environment where the subtext is, "What can I do to help you get that A?"

Back to Dave. I suppose I could have said, "What the heck were you thinking that would make you behave so appallingly back there?" That would have been a question that begins with *what*. But I'm grateful that I had the presence of mind to take the conversation off the field and collaborate with him in private. What gave me that sensitivity to the situation and the right plan of action?

I have coaches of my own, all of whom I depend on to help me get an A.

BEST: Change your mind about your role as a leader in your organization, from being a boss to being a coach.

WORST: Give in to an ego-driven impulse to demonstrate territorial superiority by chastising someone in the presence of others.

FIRST: Using the book *The Coaching Habit* as your guide, set up one-on-one conversations with your tribe members to learn from them about what they need to thrive in their roles.

Chapter 12

GRAB THE CHANCE TO MAKE A SPECTACLE OF YOURSELF

Have you heard the story of how Richard Branson once drove a British army tank through Times Square, past Rockefeller Center, all the way downtown to the New York Stock Exchange? His mission: to destroy 30 tons of Coke products for all the world to see. His ultimate purpose: to put both the planet's population and the Coca-Cola Company on notice that there was a new kid in town who would stop at nothing to crush its competition. As fate would have it, Coke crushed back and Branson's Virgin Cola venture ultimately failed. But the big New York adventure itself had staying power in the hearts and minds of business leaders over the ensuing decades who would think, *I wish I could do something like that.*

So, naturally, it was on my mind 10 years later as the WD-40 Company tribe began to brainstorm memorable ways to celebrate our upcoming 50th anniversary. Our mission: to celebrate the company, of course. Our purpose: to celebrate all the people who had been part of our story from the very beginning, from the founders, to all the tribe members over the decades, to our customers and shareholders.

Well, the tank through Manhattan thing had already been done. So that was a nonstarter. But still, Branson's example kept returning to my mind. It became a personal creative challenge for me to come up with something really good. After all, how often does a 50th birthday party come around? *Let's do it right; let's do it unforgettably,* I thought.

At that time, we were talking about the WD-40 Company as having a "fortress of brands." In the last couple of years we had acquired additional brands—like the popular 3-in-One oil—to add to the WD-40 array of offerings. And we had gotten into the habit of describing the collection as our *fortress.* Not especially glamorous, but absolutely essential to defending the company against unseen and unforeseeable market conditions. And, in the midst of brainstorming, I found myself pondering the question, "Well, who protects fortresses?" Answer: A knight does. And then the brainstorming ball began to really roll.

I said to the planning team, "How about I dress up in a suit of armor and take the formula with me to Nasdaq? We can open the Nasdaq stock exchange as a way to celebrate how the formula has delivered to the shareholders over 50 years. What about that idea?"

And then somebody said something about a horse.

"Can you ride a horse?"

"Of course I can ride a horse! I'm Australian," I replied with just a little bit of a huff for effect. Okay, so maybe not every Australian has been on a horse. And, no, I'm no stockman. And no one would mistake me for the Man from Snowy River. But still, my summers riding horses on one of my relative's dairy farms in Australia's Kiewa Valley flooded my memory. That had to count for something. In for a penny, in for a pound. No playing it safe or cutting corners. We were on. And there was no backing out for me. On the to-do list: Order a suit of armor. Oh, and find a horse to rent.

Full disclosure: We did opt out of the full suit of armor idea. But we ordered a complete set of chain mail, head to toe, as custom-made as possible to make sure it would fit this 5'11" Aussie from San Diego. And a sword. Every knight must have a sword, so we didn't forget the sword. The broad blade would be engraved to commemorate the 50th anniversary.

All told, I'm guessing the complete ensemble weighed in at about 45 pounds. I didn't drive a tank. I *wore* the tank.

We arrived in New York at 4 AM, accompanied by a team of security professionals who whispered into their sleeves about the movements and location of the "Rabbit," which was their code for the actual formula, safely encased in a see-through cube. After my dignified horseback journey from the hotel to Nasdaq headquarters, we opened the stock exchange that day, and had our picture taken in front of the big Times Square sign featuring, of course, a gigantic image of the WD-40 Multi-Use Product can. That famous blue and yellow can with the little red top had arrived in Times Square.

Outsiders, cynics even, might give us points for a clever publicity stunt—made even more remarkable by the fact that I was still able to carry a real sword through the streets of Manhattan just a couple of years after 9/11. But to me it was more than that. For me it was a gesture of love I was extending to all the WD-40 Company tribe. Everyone. Shareholders, of course. But also customers and the tribe members all over the world who had attached their own careers, fortunes, and life stories to the epic tale of WD-40 Company itself.

So what was the difference between this being a binding cultural event instead of merely a CEO's joyride and desperate bid for attention? What are the duplicable distinctions that turn this experience into a Learning Moment instead of yet another Richard Branson–level exploit?

Whatever the spectacle opportunity might be, make it about the company and its purpose, not just another wacky idea coming out of the CEO's office. For us at WD-40 Company, it was first about celebrating the accomplishment of hitting the 50th anniversary mark and all the people who poured their dedication and faith into the company over time. It was about creating a positive, lasting memory for everyone who caught wind of the entire project, from those involved in its initial planning sessions to the bystanders all along the procession route who stopped on their way to work to gawk at the knight solemnly proceeding to Times Square. Everyone was in on the joke.

Use materials within realistic reach of any average person. Granted, not everyone has access to a horse, never mind a full suit of chain mail. But it's not too difficult to figure out how to acquire such items for your planned spectacle if you really want them. The dots are connectable. Not so much the acquisition of, say, a suborbital hot air balloon or a tricked-out superyacht that is guaranteed to win any world-class race the CEO chooses to join. Or a stay on a private Caribbean island for $5,400 a night. Make it easy for everyone in your company to imagine him- or herself right there with you on the adventure.

Eliminate the potential tragedy factor. What's the worst that could happen on any given Richard Branson–type exploit? Images of international search and rescue teams combing the high seas and Sahara Desert come to mind. Grieving widows. Orphaned children. Wreaths drifting away on the waves. Maybe an untethered astronaut floating away. What was the worst that could have happened to me?

I could have tumbled off my horse and landed square on my arse at the feet of the Naked Cowboy. No tears. Just another funny story to add to the legend. I can see the headline now: "Overdressed Meets Underdressed."

Go for the joy, not for the win. There was one major flaw in Branson's tank trip: its purpose was to poke his identified major competitor—the Coca-Cola Company—in the nose. It was a story yet to unfold. And when it did finally come to a conclusion, Branson and his upstart company were the losers. So that's the story you get when you google the event. As for me and WD-40 Company? We had already "won"—we had prevailed over 50 years. And no one could take that away from us. It was time to party! We had earned it.

Make it about your people, not about yourself. On that fantastic New York day, I was just the figurehead, representing everyone. I was representing the company, not myself. I was just the bloke in a ridiculous costume, ready to go to extremes to announce to the world how proud we all are to be the WD-40 Company tribe.

Now that I'm officially Chairman Emeritus of WD-40 Company, I don't go to headquarters very often like I used to. But the sword and its scabbard are still there, encased in a protective glass box for all to see and remember and pass on the story about that day to people seeing it for the first time. Snapshots from the day are pinned to the red vest that I wore over the chain mail, helping visitors understand what happened in Manhattan that morning.

There will come a time when I no longer go to headquarters, even in my emeritus role. And all the people there will only know the story of the day the CEO rode a horse to Times Square, dressed in 45 pounds of chain mail, because someone else told them the story. Because someone else had told *those* people the story before them. The originals will be long gone. But the legend will prevail. Maybe even told during the 100th anniversary. And I imagine the story of the positive, lasting memory concluding like this:

"Really? The CEO actually did that? Why?"

"Because that's the kind of tribe we are."

BEST: Use your imagination, be original, and link the spectacle to the company's purpose.

WORST: Be mean, not meaningful. This isn't about competition. It's about celebration.

FIRST: Look for ways to include everyone in your tribe in your spectacle planning.

Chapter 13

WHAT IF YOUR WORKPLACE WAS WHERE PEOPLE ESCAPED *TO*?

One Sunday evening, in 2003, during an interview with the CBS news magazine *60 Minutes*, SAS Institute cofounder and CEO Jim Goodnight famously said something that made a world of CEOs and CHROs reflect, "Huh, I never thought of it that way before."

He said, "Ninety-five percent of my assets drive out the gate every evening. It's my job to maintain a work environment that keeps those people coming back every morning."

Of course, as a community of leaders during that time, we had already been thinking about employee engagement and employer branding as major cultural components of what some liked to call their *human capital strategy*. But in retrospect, during that time, the conversation was still a rather bloodless, intellectual, quantifiable, C-suite-based area of focus. Trends. Percentages. Cohorts. Demographics. Goodnight, for the first time, actually invited us to revisit this idea of attaching culture to the employee experience on a very, very personal level. *The individual personal experience of being a human being seeking to thrive in a workplace setting.*

Goodnight, with those two sentences, took it all the way down to this simple scenario: Every morning, in steam-covered bathroom mirrors all across the land, the decision to return to work is made freshly, all over again. And that decision will be revisited the next day. And the day after that. Behind each razor or mascara wand, eyes in the mirror are asking, "Do I go to work today or do I not? That is the question." And, if they do go, will they give it all they've got? Or will they just be there?

Yay? Or nay? The answers to those questions, day to day, all depend on how well the leadership delivers on the individual's experience of the company's employee value proposition. Or, to be more succinct, the company's culture.

Back in 2003, employers were engaged in the earlier salvos of the proverbial War for Talent. They were primarily focused on recruitment. Issues surrounding retention were important, sure, but somehow not as glamorous as stories told about the innovative ways to attract fresh talent. Pick up any issue of *Fast Company*, *Fortune*, or *Harvard Business Review* during that era and you'd be treated to examples of creative and delightful approaches to catching the attention of potential candidates. Billboards at baseball games and the promise of margarita machines, foosball tables, and skateboard parks immediately come to mind. On the other hand, employee engagement itself, as a solution to retention or recruitment, was still very much relegated to the "soft" neighborhood of HR strategy. The thrill is in the chase. Taking care of what or who you've got ... well, not so much fun. But Goodnight was telling us that we had to keep the woo machine cranked up for everyone, especially the people we assume to be already wooed and won.

Goodnight's track record made leaders stop and revisit their assumptions. In the high-tech industry that was experiencing an annual turnover rate of 20%, the turnover rate at SAS Institute was only 3%. To put a more positive spin on the statistic, in the industry overall, out of every 100 hard-won employees recruited, only 80 of them would be expected to stay year over year. At SAS, that would be 97. So here's your choice: 80? Or 97? Maybe Goodnight was on to something.

In the two decades between 2003 and 2020, Goodnight's words were certainly remembered. And they were applied here and there, to varying degrees of dedication and success. But they had become so familiar they lost that fresh edgy traction that new ideas benefit from.

It was obviously time for a refresher. And that refresher came in the form of what became known as the Great Resignation when millions of people took a good hard look in the mirror and concluded, "Nope. I'm done." As employers gradually flipped on the workplace lights when the various versions of the Covid-19 lockdown were lifted, they were dismayed to discover that too many of the workstations remained vacant. Millions of people just weren't coming back.

Come to find out, in their months of uncertainty, isolation, and, all too frequently, the personal trauma of tragic loss, people were coming to the conclusion that life is short, unpredictable, even fraught with terror at times. Even those of us who don't usually think or speak in acronyms were becoming very familiar with YOLO. You only live once. Did they really want to spend another day doing what they did in 2019?

And thus began the Great Resignation. But Whitney Johnson, author of *Disrupt Yourself: Master Relentless Change and Speed Up Your Learning Curve*, had the wisdom to ask, "What if we looked at this situation differently? What if we saw this trend as one of choice and self-agency?" In the April 6, 2022, edition of *Harvard Business Review*, she proposed that leaders move away from the despairing concept of Great Resignation and move to the more possibility-promoting idea of Great Aspiration. She wrote:

> Workers are aspiring to proactively make the life they want . . . [T]he Great Resignation appellation is, I believe, mistaken. Most workers are not simply quitting. They are following a dream re-fined in pandemic adversity. They are aspiring to grow in the ways most important to them.

What if we met our tribe members where they were, which was on their way to something even better? And we gave *that* to them?

Wouldn't you rather create a workplace where those who are on the Great Aspiration journey see value in being part of your tribe? Especially if the alternative is to be a workplace that is constantly pursuing those who have already left in spirit, if not in fact (those quiet quitters)? If we are to take on the assumption that our people *voluntarily* engage with us in the workplace, it's up to us to offer them what they're seeking in order to keep them coming back for more.

What other population already engages with us voluntarily and successfully? Customers, of course. How do we know our relation-ship with them is a successful one? Because they *choose* to return for more. They have identified our value proposition as the one that helps them achieve the desired result—whether it be self-actualization or clear skin. Preferably packaged in a reasonably easy-to-use product delivery system. Isn't that the dynamic that we want to offer our tribe members, per Goodnight and Johnson?

What if we had a workplace culture in which we didn't worry about the Great Resignation because our tribe experience was one that people ran *to* instead of away *from*?

Who are the experts in getting their target demographic to immediately identify the product promise, give it a try, and then come back again and again? Brand experts. Let's take a look at just a few of the many core components of a brand—its positioning, promise, and delivery—and consider the workplace corollaries.

A well-articulated and proven performance promise: Go shopping for a box of Band-Aids, for instance, and you'll likely find the Band-Aids (assuming you're in the right store). It's unlikely that you'll put a can of motor oil in your basket by mistake. Product developers know—because they thought this through and did customer research—that a successful Band-Aid will give the customers what they want: a sterile piece of gauze to protect the cut and a reliable adhesive that will secure the strip to the skin, yet is easy to remove later. And that's what they deliver in a readily identifiable box.

Leaders know what their preferred tribe members want out of their employment experience. Generally speaking, people thrive in an environment where they can devote their energies, time, and brain power to a cause that's important to them. They want an environment where they are physically and emotionally safe. They want to know that they are building a future for themselves, growing into their own full potential. They want to know they matter and they want to feel like they belong. They know they can find those attributes in the employment opportunities you offer. Leaders are explicit in their leadership and cultural messaging. And they deliver on the experience in a clearly labeled package.

Explicitly expressed values that all tribe members (both employees and customers) can align themselves with: Well-written and frequently communicated company values are relevant to everyone who voluntarily engages with the business. They are a point of pride and emotional bonding that transcends the transactional relationship. They serve the cause and purpose of the business, the customer, and the employee over and above the mere exchange of money or time.

The unspoken message here is, "My choice to be a part of this tribe helps me be proud of who I am." There are many opportunities to build emotional connections with the tribe through clearly expressed and defined values: the purpose and set of beliefs that drive every aspect of the brand journey; the ways leaders are trained to inspire and coach their tribe members; volunteerism; the company's code of ethics; social responsibility; the way leaders manage the inevitable interpersonal conflicts when they come up; the ways customers and employees describe what the company means to them over and above the product it delivers to the marketplace.

Consistency and authenticity in the product delivery for both customers and tribe members: Employees in the hospitality industry know this dichotomy all too well. You're probably familiar with the concepts of "front of house" and "back of house." In a restaurant, for instance, the areas that a guest experiences are well-appointed, clean, gracious, luxurious to the extent that reflects the brand promise. That's the front of the house. Open one of those heavy doors leading to the back of the house and it's an entirely different story. Scuffed and dirty cinder block walls. Hallways filled with heavy, noisy metal racks and carts. Bright lights. The contrast is jarring, even at a glance through the rapidly shutting door as a waiter disappears. And, of course, it's a functional necessity. The back of the house can't be luxuriously carpeted and comfortable.

But that doesn't mean that the staff can't be treated as graciously and thoughtfully by their leaders as their leaders expect them to treat the guests. Maybe in different ways. But the spirit must be the same. Where there's a break in the consistency and authenticity, there's a break in the chain of goodwill and trust.

Martha Finney, my collaborator on this book and author of *The Truth About Getting the Best from People*, tells the story of her first such experience. After graduating from college, she moved to New York City to write for a celebrity environmentalist whose focus was on the oceans and marine mammals. Her employer told her that her salary would be significantly below market because, as a nonprofit, all the money went to the cause for which the organization was celebrated around the world.

"Living in Manhattan made the income-to-expense balance really difficult, especially by month's end," she recalls. "But I always made it work, because, you know, the baby seals and everything.

"That all came to a screeching halt my first (and only) Christmas with the organization," she continues. "The first Monday after the holidays, the office manager came swanning into the office twirling around in a full-length fur coat. 'Look what our boss gave me for Christmas!' she said. 'It's mink. Next year I hope it's a seal coat.'

"I soon gave my two-week notice," she says. "The reasons, of course, were multiple. It wasn't so much that my celebrity boss had given her an extremely extravagant gift. That was between the two of them. Although, to be honest, the gap between her gift and the office staff was unignorable—the rest of us each received the same thing—a crock of middling 'gourmet' mustard from his home country. Probably purchased at the D'Agostino's down the block. I wondered if it would go well with my packets of ramen noodles.

"What disengaged me right then and there was a breach of several values promises: Those of us who were willing to sacrifice for the sake of the seals were unlikely to celebrate any gift made of fur, no matter what the cost. Her taunting us by saying that she hoped the next year would net her a seal coat was a direct spit in the eye of the entire mission of the organization and the value of our personal sacrifices. Not to mention the sacrifices of all the individuals who wrote checks to the organization at their kitchen tables, And, let's face it, her flaunting the fur around the office the way she did was just plain bad manners. That was the moment I quit in spirit. Didn't take me long to quit in fact.

"But even then I knew I benefited from the experience. That episode was one of the first hints that my own life's work would be about building the body of knowledge around positive workplace experiences, not abusive ones. To use Whitney Johnson's vernacular, I suppose I owe this nonprofit a debt of gratitude because it helped me define my aspiration. Which never changed since that day."

Every day, millions of Marthas around the world ask themselves, "Does my experience with this organization align with my aspirations?" Maybe not in so many words. But the outcome of the answer is always the same—another question: "Do I stay or do I go?"

BEST: Welcome this insight that you can make the workplace environment one that attracts and keeps cherished tribe members who are devoted to your organization's cause.

WORST: Assume that a competitive job market or bad economy will keep your tribe members loyal to your business.

FIRST: Find out what emotional rewards your tribe members want from their experience with your organization. And then dedicate your efforts to delivering on those expectations.

Chapter 14

MAKE YOUR WORKPLACE A MENTAL HEALTH REFUGE

By the time you read this—about a year after these words were written—the world might have turned completely upside down. Or maybe it's right side back up again. There's no real way to know for certain at this particular moment. In fact, news out of Taiwan overnight reminds us that everything can change in the blink of an eye. Or the click of a mouse. Or the post of a tweet.

In the late-night hours in the US time zones of April 2, 2024, Twitter (are we finally calling it X now, future readers?) followers of a young American reporter are enjoying her post about how much she's relishing her fresh morning coffee on the 21st floor of her Taiwanese apartment, looking out over the skyline of Taichung City. "Good morning!" she crows to the world as she posts a picture of skyscrapers in front of a mountain range. As for her coffee, she writes proudly, "I think I've earned it." Maybe she had just put in her steps and reps at the gym downstairs. So, yes, if that's the case, she certainly did.

Minutes later she writes this: "I have never been so terrified in my life. This earthquake is very serious. I thought we were going to die. I am [sic] cannot stop shaking. This earthquake is a bad one. Oh. God."

An hour later: "Another aftershock right now. I may not survive this . . ."

A 7.4 earthquake had just hit Taiwan that morning between sips from her coffee cup. She posted tweets between aftershocks, each one shaking her confidence that she would be alive one minute longer. Her US friends tracked each one of her posts like they might track labor contractions, holding their breath as they waited for the next one. And then the next. Until she finally reported that she was signing off to sort out what was left of her life high up on the 21st floor—the coffee, one would suppose, either forgotten or spilled all over the floor in front of the once beautiful window showcasing once spectacular scenery. Only now it's devastation.

(As of this writing, 13 are dead, 100 are missing. None of whom had expected the day to turn out that way as they went through their morning routines. Many of whom were on their way to work when the world shook the streets.)

CEOs around the world can be forgiven if the first question—well, maybe the second question—that came to mind was "How will this affect my semiconductor chip order?" For individuals all over the world, it's yet another incident, among so many of them since 2001, where we are reminded that in a single instant it can all go to smash.

As you're reading this months later, you might be thinking, *Oh, how quaint and young we were in 2024. It's a good thing we didn't know what was coming our way,* or *Thank God these bad times are behind us.* In any case, we are learning in new ways the same lessons we learned during 9/11 and the Covid lockdowns: how vital human connection is to our mental health and the human spirit. Even on the 21st floor of a Taiwan apartment building surrounded by earthquake rubble and mayhem, this one reporter received comfort from the knowledge that she was connected to everyone she cared about and who cared for her all over the world. Her coworkers. "Keep writing to us," a colleague implored. "That way we'll know you're safe." And she did. Hour after hour.

Connection. She was surrounded by people and prayers around the globe. And she knew it. It saw her through a terrible first day of earthquake and aftershocks, each one carrying the possibility of being the one that ends it all. She was alone. But not alone. And that was the source of her strength.

In the previous chapter I invited you to reconsider the concept of the Great Resignation and imagine what it would be like if your workplace offered employees the experience of *fulfilling their aspirations*.

Now I'd like to invite you to look at how your workplace can also be a mentally healthy refuge of community, connection, belonging, and the essential belief that there is still good to be done in the world. In the company of kindred spirits, all sharing the same goal, vision, and dream. And we're the ones lucky enough to do it! No matter what mayhem might be raging outside our doors.

Mental health in these times is a crucial consideration for leaders all over the world. Anxiety alone is invading our work and workplace to the point where authors Chester Elton and Adrian Gostick call it a pandemic in their book *Anxiety at Work: 8 Strategies to Help Teams Build Resilience, Handle Uncertainty, and Get Stuff Done*. They write:

> In a 2018 survey, 34 percent of workers of all ages reported feeling anxiety at least once in the previous month, and 18 percent

had a diagnosed anxiety disorder . . . Harvard Medical School research claimed on-the-job anxiety imperils workers' careers and company productivity. Anxiety is leading to increased employee errors, growing burnout, workplace rage, more sick days, and poor employee health . . . Worry, stress, and resulting anxiety at work can cause employees to lose focus and withdraw, working at a reduced capacity and rebuffing attempts by fellow team members or managers to help.

And this was reported *before* Covid, the lockdowns, the deaths, diseases of despair, inflation, social upheaval, earthquakes, and all the currently unpredictable things that will have happened by the time you read this chapter.

As it turns out, one key to mental health is having a job to do, in the companionship of others who are also single-mindedly committed to the same goal, all with the belief within our grasp that we have the necessary capabilities, tools, and time to achieve that goal. The emotionally healthy tribal environment sets that up for us. That's your job.

Martin Seligman, whom most of us know as the father of positive psychology, has most recently been focusing on the concept of *flourishing*, which he describes this way: "To flourish is to find fulfillment in our lives, accomplishing meaningful and worthwhile tasks, and connecting with others at a deeper level—in essence, living the 'good life.'" The mental health advantages result in these outcomes:*

- Fewer missed days of work
- Fewer half-days and work cutbacks

---

* Source: https://positivepsychology.com/flourishing/#factors-flourishing.

- Lower sense of helplessness
- More clear life goals
- Higher resilience
- Higher intimacy
- Lower risk of cardiovascular disease
- Lower number of chronic physical diseases with age
- Fewer health limitations of daily living activities
- Lower health care utilization

The tribe member benefits. And so does the tribe as a whole.

Coincidentally (or not), all five of the components Seligman says are essential for flourishing can be found in the tribal workplace setting. He details these in his book *Flourish: A Visionary New Understanding of Happiness and Well-Being* with an easy-to-remember acronym, PERMA: positive emotions, engagement, relationships, meaning, and achievement. In your workplace culture, these components can look like this:

- **Positive emotions:** Your tribe members enjoy working together. They enjoy playing together. They relish healthy competition. They laugh. They even cry together in mutual support. They know their goals are within reach. They are hopeful that their efforts will be rewarded with accomplishment and celebration. They belong to each other and will do almost anything to help each other succeed. And they know that they can count on others to do the same for them.
- **Engagement:** Your tribe members care about their work, their customers, and their fellow tribe members. They have confidence in the company's future. They have what they need in terms of tools, education, and support from their

coaches to get the job done. They can focus fully on the work in front of them, feeling safe and secure that their tribe wants their success too.

- **Relationships:** Your tribe members feel deeply connected to the people they work with and see every day. They care about each other beyond the parameters of their roles in the tribe. They know they can trust their fellow tribe members to speak the truth and look out for them in uncertain, sometimes even dangerous, times. They seek each other out for emotional support, collaboration, even just plain fun.

- **Meaning:** Your tribe members believe in the mission behind what they do, the products they make, the customers they serve. They know how their work makes the world a better place. When they're asked what they do in social settings, they speak to that ultimate mission rather than focus simply on their skills or job description.

- **Achievement:** Your tribe members can reasonably expect to be successful meeting their goals, completing their tasks, and watching how the world benefits from their efforts.

As I write this, it's April 2024. When are you reading it? In a year's time? Two years? Five years? What does your world look like now? Does it bear any resemblance at all to what you remember April 2024 to have been like? I hope so, in a good way.

But as you look back on the months and years that have come before, think back on the times when you felt the most focused, serene in concentration, accomplished, joyful, celebratory, taken care of, safe.

Well, I hope many of those times have been with your family.

But I also hope that working in the company of your tribe comes in second. A very, very close second.

And that you, as their coach, provided those same feelings for the people who look to you for leadership.

BEST: Resolve to make your workplace environment an emotionally supportive refuge from external conditions that only harm your people's mental health.

WORST: Believe that people should leave their personal problems in the parking lot before coming to work.

FIRST: As a tribe, study the PERMA acronym and consider all the different ways your workforce supports those five elements. Then look for ways the community of colleagues can promote the PERMA elements in their behaviors and experiences with each other.

"IF YOU CAN'T MAKE THEM HAPPY, AT LEAST DON'T HURT THEM"

Chapter 15

WITH GREAT DISRUPTION COMES THE MESSY MIDDLE

Look at any resume or CV within easy reach of where you're sitting right now. Let's say it's yours. You'll see the expected elements: name, address, contact information, a succession of companies. You'll also see the predictable bullet lists of titles, roles, tasks, accomplishments. This is where it gets interesting to me. Most people look at those bullet points as indicators of what the resume holder has achieved and therefore, by implication, can achieve for the next employer. Checked boxes, of qualifications, so to speak.

I see them differently. I see each bullet point as the place where you are saying, "This is where I was willing to step away from the comfort zone and show myself to be a dumb-ass all over again."

Each bullet point is like a capsule. It holds the question: "Can I pull this off? Or is this where my luck might run out?"

In addition to the obvious achievement, each bullet point holds a story of vulnerability and courage. The willingness to transform yet again, with one more adventure into the unknown. The acquisition of one more skill or experience that will mature you into an ever-wiser leader. Come what may, failure or success. Well, naturally, a resume will most likely show just the successes. But those failures also hold very interesting stories about how you, the adventurer, were willing to step up and do unfamiliar things in strange places. In, very likely, full view of others who are looking on and coming to their own conclusions about what a dumb-ass you might be.

With each adventure there is always that possibility that you will meet with your terminal dumb-assery; that you will have found the farthest frontier of your ability to take on a new challenge. And the failure might be a permanent definition of all your limitations.

Or you can do what I've done and take on each new opportunity with the attitude of, "I'll give it a go."

Up until the point in my career when I moved from Australia to San Diego, the significant changes and decisions I had made were natural growth spurts. Not always comfortable, very often challenging. But I knew that with each step I would be in good company, in a good company, surrounded by mentors and coaches who sincerely wanted to contribute to my success. I never lost sight of how fortunate I was as I stepped up the ranks of opportunity.

WD-40 Company was to play a part in the two most disruptive changes of my career story. The first came from a fax delivered overnight through the machine I had stashed under my bed (I was working from home at the time—that's how small potatoes I was then), assigning to me the task of starting up WD-40 Company Australia. It would be up to my 31-year-old self to stand up an entire corporation with only that horrible piece of thermal paper in my hand as my starting point. With me standing there in my pajamas. I had to do all the things: find office space, identify and hire the necessary staff, and make sure all the legal and regulatory issues were identified and handled before it would be too late.

Did I know how to do any of those things? No. But I knew who to call for each opened question. And I knew enough to know that I needed to reach out for help at every turn. And so I did. Within six months, WD-40 Company (Australia) Pty Ltd was officially launched.

The next disruption was also ignited inauspiciously, this time with a simple phone call. After WD-40 Company Australia was successfully launched, I found I had some bandwidth in my days, enough energy, focus, and eagerness to learn new things. So I called Jerry Schlief, the CEO at the time.

I said, "I can take on more projects at this point. What else would you like me to do for WD-40 Company?"

Jerry responded, "Funny you should ask. Your name came up the other day."

And with that, I began my next disruption: the relocation from my lifelong homeland to San Diego, California, to take on the assignment of bringing WD-40 Company to the global marketplace. With my wife and young family supporting me, I said "Goodbye, for now" to my friends and family and all the details involved in day-to-day living that I knew so well. And I started again.

The big questions were handled by experts and staffers, all of whom sincerely wanted to support my success. Where I would be working. What my compensation would be. What successful goal achievement would look like and how it would be quantified. Where I would be living. I had already acquired the appropriate visa to work in the United States. How would I acquire my green card? How to get a driver's license and learn to drive on the opposite side of the road? Oh no! How to find a house or buy a car without an official US-based credit rating?

Here's what really tripped me up: running into people in the hallways. Did you know that Americans automatically walk on the right side in their office corridors? Americans drive on the right, so it's to be expected that they would naturally walk on the right. Likewise, escalators are set up in opposite directions than I was used to. Where I would seek out the up escalator, I would find the down escalator. I had to discover those details for myself. More than once, I'm afraid, before the lessons sank in.

And here's one for you—I kept missing my desired exits on the interstate. Here I am, this executive bloke who is tasked with the mandate to set up a domestic company for success all over the world. And I can't even get back home at the end of the day without having to double back on the interstate to return to the exit I just flew by. Just like I did the day before. And the day before that. Why did this keep happening? Because Americans install those little green signs displaying exit numbers *on the top* of the large interstate signs. Not the bottom, like they do in Australia. My Aussie brain was wired to look at the bottom. Every time. Considering the price of gas in San Diego, when I think of all the money I wasted doubling back over and over again, I wonder what kind of car I would have been able to make payments on with that extra cash.*

Live and learn, as they say. Whitney Johnson puts it more elegantly. She says, "Jump on that S curve and ride the wave."

We are living in an era of accelerating disruption—as you manage the S curve waves of learning and mastering, you will not only cope, but also harness the power and unpredictability of

---

* As we were developing this chapter, my writing partner, Martha Finney, and I discovered yet another new thing about those little exit number signs. If it is positioned on the right side of the sign, the exit ramp will appear on the right lane. If the little exit sign is fastened on the left upper edge of the larger sign, that's your cue to move over to the left lane where you'll soon find the exit ramp. Learn something new every day.

disruption to catapult you forward. If you want to be successful in unexpected ways, follow your own disruptive path. Dare to innovate. Do something astonishing. Disrupt yourself.

In *Disrupt Yourself*, Johnson brilliantly describes the disruption experience as an S curve. When you align the shape of the S with any kind of innovation or personal disruption, it goes roughly this way: The bottom plane is where you start the transition. You are at a level of comfort and competence, even mastery, in your current situation. When you are ready to "dare to innovate," you climb the upward trajectory toward the next horizontal line, which is both your landing place and your launching place for your next disruption, should you choose to take on the challenge.

That upward sloping line is where all the adventure lies. Where you'll meet new people, learn new skills, discover new frontiers of your dumb-assery. Johnson writes:

> Self-disruption will force you up steep foothills of new information, relationships, and systems. The looming mountain may seem insurmountable, but the S curve helps us understand that if we keep working at it, we can reach that inflection point where our understanding and competence will suddenly shoot upward. This is the fun part of disruption, rapidly scaling to new heights of success and achievement. Eventually, you will plateau and your growth will taper off. Then it's time to look for new ways to disrupt.

Are you game for the ride? Do you want to keep transforming and growing year over year? Be willing to reveal your inner dumbass, expose yourself to new opportunities to risk failure but maybe also learn new skills, ways, and approaches to life and work?

As a leader you can take heart in knowing that you're not the only dumb-ass in the hallways. Because upheaval is surrounding us all in one way or the other, everyone you meet is likely to be on some kind of S curve in their lives. Especially new hires in your organization, who are trying to appear confident but are wondering, "Can I pull this off?" Notice the new dumb-ass in your organization and kindly offer to show that person the ways of the company and culture. You're not making friends with someone who is innately stupid or clumsy. You're making friends with someone who is courageously trying new things in a new environment and managing the stress of it all by taking the journey up the S curve one day at a time.

I was that person. I was surrounded by a lot of support. And I will never forget the kindness of the people who welcomed me into my new country and sincerely wished success for me.

BEST: Welcome the discomfort that comes with disruption, either in yourself or in your tribe members. Celebrate that upward trajectory on the S curve as the messy middle, which is where you'll discover all sorts of Learning Moments—personal, professional, and organizational.

WORST: Expect perfection in performance and delivery all the time, from both yourself and the people you lead.

FIRST: Be the first one in your organization to publicly say, "I don't know how to do this new thing. Does anyone have any advice for me?"

Chapter 16

HOW TO BE THE LEADER PEOPLE LOVE TO LOATHE

What inspires an enduring fondness for companies like WD-40 Company? On a consumer level, of course, it's the quality of the product and the brand messaging that surrounds it. Our blue and yellow can with the little red top isn't the kind of purchase that causes new owners to say to their friends, "Have you seen my new acquisition?" as if it were a painting or dream car in the garage. It's a humble, friendly little thing that patiently waits in a cupboard or on a workshop shelf for those moments when it's needed. You don't have to save up for it. Or dress up for it. You just reach for it, aim that red smart straw at the trouble spot, give it a spray, and breathe a sigh of relief that, "Yes! Once again, it works perfectly."

Investors also enjoy its performance. But in a different way. In November 1997, the first month of my term as CEO, the WD-40 Company stock price was $29. On my retirement in September 2022, the WD-40 Company stock price was $185.69. Shareholders who owned the stock over that period certainly benefited from the great culture that was the driver of execution of the global strategy, which was to take the blue and yellow can with the little red top to the world.

Tribe members love companies like WD-40 Company because the culture allows them to do the work they enjoy with people whose company they enjoy, for a cause they believe in, and then go home happy to enjoy their families. Year over year, WD-40 Company's engagement scores demonstrate that the leadership must be doing multiple things correctly to sustain its tribe members' fondness for the workplace that breathes life into the company itself.

"Fondness," of course, in leadership circles, is called "employee engagement," a subject of inquiry that lends itself handily to being quantified. So, as with most world-class companies, WD-40 Company asks its tribe members every year how they're feeling, thinking about, and experiencing the company. At WD-40 Company, it's called the Employee Engagement Index. Over the years, we narrowed the survey items down to 26. And then we distribute it to everyone around the world, translated into seven languages. Here are some of my favorite 2022 results, which was my last year as CEO:

"I love to tell people that I work for WD-Company."	98%
"I am excited about WD-40 Company's future direction."	94%
"I know what results are expected of me."	96%
"I feel my opinions and values are a good fit with the WD-40 Company culture."	97%
"I respect my coach."	97%

All of these answers are experience-based. The way the tribe members experience their time at WD-40 Company shapes their perceptions of the company, and whether they continuously feel it is a good place for them to invest their time, talents, passion, and, hopefully, their entire careers.

———

So here we have three different populations whose positive opinions are extremely important to any company that wants to succeed: consumers, investors, employees. When it comes to leadership considerations, here's the most important difference that separates employees from the other two: consumer and investor fondness for the company is something that is built over time, measured quarter by quarter, year over year, generation after generation. There is resilience in the company's success and, by and large, forgiveness in occasional slipups and hits to the reputation.

The employee's allegiance to the company, however, is built up every time trust is confirmed. But the whole relationship—as it's perceived in terms of the culture—can come tumbling down with just one breach of the cultural promise between the leadership and the tribe.

Leadership behaviors are the essential building blocks of the day-to-day culture experience of the entire company community. It's one thing to identify and celebrate leaders who seem to have the magic touch, the charisma that makes everyone confident that they are safe, they belong, and they matter. But it's also educational to consider what the characteristics are of a leader whose behaviors create the exact opposite of the ideal workplace environment.

And so, I imagined my old friend Alec (or it could be Alice), the Soul-Sucking CEO. And I'd like to introduce him or her to you right now. You will likely recognize Alec from the behaviors I describe here. Hopefully in someone else, not yourself!

Alec has no compelling purpose: As it turns out, having a clearly defined purpose that speaks to the hearts and minds of employees is actually critical to creating an engaged culture where your people know they belong among kindred spirits who are passionate about serving a cause larger than themselves. Alec just talks in terms of market share, competition, and money. There is no sense of larger contribution to society or the world that inspires the hearts and minds of everyone who is associated with the business. Purpose-driven, passionate people guided by strong values create amazing outcomes. Having a purpose is highly motivating. Purpose is soul-enriching, not soul-sucking. Purpose motivates people to feel part of something where they believe that they are making a difference.

Having no compelling purpose is an active disadvantage in the sense that there's a vacuum in focus and direction. That vacuum is going to be filled by absolutely the wrong things. You'll find yourself creating unsuccessful products that don't serve your customers. You'll have a workplace where people treat each other in a way that's shabby and disrespectful. The vacuum creates space for rumormongering, interrelationship suspicions and conflicts, and other destructive issues.

Alec doesn't communicate in terms of positive values: Without positive values, people require micromanagement and constant course correction. They will be made to feel fundamentally wrong from the minute they turn off their alarm clock in the morning to the time they drag their depleted bodies back up the front walk to their house in the evening. Without values, they can't be trusted to make decisions on their own. And they will know it. They are exposed to danger, and they know their company is exposed. Any day, some horrible headline about some unethical behavior committed by an executive will cause the whole company to come crashing down.

The worst thing that can happen in an organization is someone getting really good results and violating values. Inevitably, people conclude that "It's results at all costs and values don't matter." That will kill your company over the long term. It demoralizes your people, depletes energy, squanders confidence, burns up the sense of belonging inside your culture. It creates friction among tribe members and employees. People start doing really bad things; they hurt each other and your customers, just to get results. It stops being about treating people with respect and dignity.

Values create freedom for purpose-driven talent to do their work well and independently. They are the written reminders of behaviors that we want within the business that protect both the people and the business. They also give people the freedom to be able to make decisions without having to beg for permission up the hierarchy all the time.

A strong culture based on values also sets the stage for innovation and marketplace advantage because you now have employees who are not using their precious brain cells worrying about unexpected ways they might mess up. They're free to innovate and create market-differentiating, competitive ideas.

Alec lets ego override empathy: Instead of treating people with respect and dignity, instead of showing vulnerability and humility, Alec might as well put a sign on his office door (always closed, of course) that reads: "I am the King of the World. Everyone, bow down." He separates himself from those he leads.

Alec is all about Alec. He doesn't take the time to truly understand what his people need to stay inspired and motivated. Alec doesn't know—or care about—what they need to be whole in their entire lives, to feel fulfilled in every aspect of their experiences.

Ego-driven, Alec always wants to speak first. He wants to tell; he doesn't want to ask. He wants to own every idea, even—or especially—if it means taking credit away from the person who originated it. Alec always wants to have his stamp on every idea, every project, every success.

Alec is short-term and reaction driven: The vision-crushing ritual of quarterly earnings is not the measure of long-term success in any organization. Being continuously driven by the reward of the short term will suck the soul from the organization. Efforts to build an enduring, positive, and effective culture take years to make a difference.

By focusing exclusively on the short term, Alec cripples any ability for his people to plan confidently for the future, for both the business and their family. And then they take that feeling home to their families where they struggle to raise hopeful, empowered children.

Alec creates a culture where people are driven by fear of their managers. Fear is the most disabling emotion we have. Yet bad things happen in companies. It's just a fact of life. When people are afraid to try new things, make a mistake now and then, despite the best of intentions, fear precludes creativity and freedom.

Alec doesn't keep promises: Alec has a track record of breaking promises. And it sends two soul-sucking messages to employees:

1. Anyone's word inside the corporate culture doesn't amount to much. Not only is the leader's word worthless; no one is expected to be accountable for their commitments. Breaking promises is a culturally accepted norm.

2. When tribe members are on the receiving end of broken promises, the unspoken message here is that they aren't worthy of the leader's respect. That's also soul-sucking. The only way they can continue to function inside this culture is simply to not expect honorable interaction from their leadership and coworkers. Expectations are too high. Their hearts will break. Then they go home and kick the dog.

Alec hoards information: Knowledge is power. We all know that. With all the critical knowledge safely tucked away, Alec is now truly king of the hill because he knows everything. Alec's ego is more important than the tribe.

Employees who suspect that their leader is withholding valuable information experience the slow leaking of their spirits, confidence, and dedication to the company's success. That's because they don't feel like *their* success is your number one priority. A true soul-enriching leader is intent upon helping each person step into the best version of their personal self every day. And that requires a full, respectful sharing of the information necessary for your people to perform at their top potential. Every day.

One of my favorite quotes—which we'll dive into more deeply in the epilogue—comes from Aristotle: "Pleasure in the job puts perfection in the work." Our job as leaders is to put pleasure in the job for our employees, not suck the soul from our people. In my own personal experience, pleasure in my job empowers higher quality in the work I do. And I see evidence of the same in all the people I work with—clients, colleagues, collaborators. It's about creating an opportunity for meaningful work, which is in itself a pleasure to perform. And then the result is a company that meets—even exceeds—all its essential goals among all the populations that are so important to us.

Will you commit to being the leader who prioritizes creating a joyful workplace culture? If you choose not to, that is certainly your prerogative. And, sadly, you'll have plenty of company. Just bear in mind that the people you pass in your hallways or meet in your cafeteria might be looking for a new job.

BEST: Commit to being the opposite of Alec. Consider all the behaviors associated with what it takes to be Alec, brainstorm their direct opposite behaviors, and promise yourself and your tribe that you will be that leader instead.

WORST: Refuse to apologize for violating your values as a leader. We're all human, and we all slip up. We all need to ask for forgiveness every now and then. Don't shrug off a misstep with the rationalization that "they'll get over it." They won't.

FIRST: Dedicate time to seriously consider how you want to be known as a leader. Use the Soul-Sucking CEO framework as your brainstorming prompts. How exactly will those opposite behaviors look when you put them into action yourself? What conditions or circumstances might tempt you away from your commitment to be the leader you want to be? How can you avoid them, or rectify them before it's too late? Plan and imagine now for future potential blindsides.

Chapter 17

DON'T IGNORE THE ALARM BELLS (EVEN THE FALSE ONES)

If you're like me, a sizable portion of your life is spent on the road. Travel is just a fact of leadership life these days. And, if you're like me, you still enjoy the discoveries and delights of distant lands. New friends, new cultures, new cuisine. (Although there was that time when I had to gulp down what could only be best described as snot in a shot glass; the word *delicacy* should have tipped me off before I committed.)

And also if you're like me, you maintain your mental health by installing points of familiarity here and there throughout the world where you know you don't have to make new decisions or politely grimace through unfamiliar tastes and textures. Where you can just flop into the reassuring lap of routine and take a breather from all the excitement.

For me, one of those points of familiarity is a lovely, friendly hotel in London. I try to go there every time I visit that city. It used to be a predictable 30 minutes from Heathrow by cab. (These days, it only takes 15 minutes, thanks to the Heathrow Express.) Since I know the scenery en route by heart, I can simply rest my eyes until we pull up to the door. I know the hotel's ways. I know the doorman. He knows me. Reception calls me by name. Not in the upper-crust "ladies and gentlemen serving ladies and gentlemen" kind of way. But in a "Hello, mate! We've all been looking forward to seeing you again!" kind of way. They know my favorite rooms and try to reserve one for me when they see my name come up in the reservations system. People being kind and thoughtful to kind and thoughtful people. Largely because that's the way they are with everyone. But also because they know me by name. And I know them by name.

Which makes the story I'm about to tell all the more embarrassing.

One cold and drizzly November night in London, I was especially looking forward to an early evening in my hotel room after a grueling trip that had included San Diego, Sydney, Perth, Shanghai, and now London. A full day of meetings in London followed. So now it was a well-earned evening in my room watching British comedy and enjoying a couple of beers (Stella Artois, to be precise) that I had bought in the store across from the hotel. For dinner: a simple carryout order of good warm curry and rice. I got into a fresh set of T-shirt and shorts, and comfortably settled in for the evening. Heaven.

Only this time: *Brrrrrrrrrrrrrrrrrrrringggggggg!* And the red alarm light annoyingly started flashing on the wall. "Gosh, that's loud," I grumbled to myself as I pointed the remote control to the TV to increase the volume.

Again: *Brrrrrrrrrrrrrrrrrrrringggggggg!*

And again: *Brrrrrrrrrrrrrrrrrrrrrrringgggggg!* And again. And again. In increasingly rapid succession.

Now this is beginning to get really annoying, I thought, as I loaded up my fork with another bite of curry, and tried to ignore the flashing red light. Having stayed in many hotels, I had heard many alarms over the years. My life experience up until that evening had told me that the alarm would be turned off in a matter of minutes, and management would apologize over loudspeaker. So I did what I usually do (or did)—I ignored this one too. What seasoned traveler hasn't had to endure a false alarm in a hotel at least once? And, after all, I was a seasoned traveler, I thought. I knew a false alarm when I heard one. Let the others scramble to the lobby in whatever they happened to be wearing. I, for one, would not be letting my dinner grow cold.

These false alarms need to be attended to, I thought. *They're harming the guest experience of the hotel. Especially this time of night when there might be people trying to sleep. A man can't even eat in peace. I should have a word with management in the morning.*

Then: *Bang! Bang! Bang!* Someone in the hallway was calling my name between the poundings on my door.

"Mr. Ridge! Mr. Ridge! Please leave your room immediately. Leave! Leave! Leave! We are evacuating the premises! Now!"

Now they had my attention. I put down my fork and grabbed my cell phone and passport. I slid my feet into those undersized slippers that come with these kinds of hotels, and walked down six flights of stairs to the ground floor.

I soon found myself standing outside the hotel (not even in the warm confines of the lobby), along with everyone else. The difference between them and me? Because they had complied with the first alarm, they had time to find their coat and shoes. I, however, did not. This seasoned traveler was standing outside on a cold, damp London sidewalk wearing just his undershirt, shorts, and bare feet slid into thin hotel slippers.

Police and sniffer dogs were everywhere. We were directed down the street and instructed to wait in an open park space in Berkeley Square. So much for my warm room, beer, and British comedy.

Within the hour, as we stood out there in the park, it began to rain. Finally we were allowed to return to the hotel, cold, wet, miserable, and curious. What had happened? It was indeed a false alarm. Someone had left a backpack in the hotel lobby. And management wisely erred on the side of caution, concluding that it might be a bomb. So evacuation was in order.

How stupid I had been to ignore the initial alarm. If I'd simply complied with the first alert, I would have had the time and presence of mind to dress more appropriately for the London night. Upon further reflection, I realized that there were likely many alarm bells in my life, personally and professionally, that I was choosing to ignore. On the long flight back to San Diego, I started to list all the warning signs and signals I could think of, and there were many, as I would discover. I was 20 pounds overweight, to start with. And I certainly didn't get enough exercise. More importantly, I didn't tell my loved ones that I love them often enough. I've been told that I don't listen well or enough. And what global signals might I be missing that could affect the company? What if oil went to $100 a barrel? It was then about $50 a barrel. (As of this writing, 19 years later, it's at $80.90. And in June 2022, it was $122 a barrel. So it's wise to keep up with such things!)

I hate to admit it but I allowed myself to fall into the trap of my own normalcy bias. And I got caught with my pants down. Well, *off* would be a better word to use, if you want to get technical about it.

When the words "I've been in this situation before; I know better" cross your mind, that should be your cue to look alive. And reach for your passport and shoes. And pants.

Relying on our past experiences to give us the horse sense we need to guide us in current circumstances is human nature. That's what experience is for. It's a time-, energy-, and labor-saving device that helps us make a multitude of wise decisions throughout the day. But if we let our experience-based self-preening have the last word without employing fresh thinking and new inquiry, that's when we get into trouble. Let me rephrase: That's when we get *ourselves* into trouble.

When we ignore the alarm bells, this is what can happen . . .

We can talk ourselves into rationalizing away evidence of cracks in the culture. An especially valuable and cherished tribe member decides to leave the company. At first you're shocked by the news; maybe you even feel that your trust has been betrayed. But upon reflection, you begin to remember moments when that person tried to tell you what has been happening deep inside the organization. If you had only stopped to truly listen, would you have been able to fix the problems before losing the essential tribe member?

We can miss an opportunity to leverage an unmet need in the marketplace. If it's not broken, don't fix it, right? Well, not necessarily. If you have the reputation of being someone who likes things just the way they are, your people might not be motivated to volunteer innovation and great ideas in brainstorming meetings. If your guiding principle is, "If it's not broken, don't fix it," their guiding principle might be, "What you don't know won't hurt you." The *you*, in this case, would be you. And yes, you would be hurt. You might not realize it until it's too late.

We run the risk of underestimating external threats. False alarms are a fact of life. Mark Twain famously said, "I've had a lot of worries in my life, most of which never happened." We know how unnecessary stress and anxiety can distract us and deplete our energies. But what calamities have interrupted your life that you hadn't anticipated? We try to sort out those wasteful worries, set them aside, and pick the concerns that we judge to be the most legitimate issues to focus on. Mark Twain would approve. But then again, what's lurking in the discard pile that has been sending you signals that you simply chose to ignore?

We leave ourselves vulnerable to manipulations by our competitors, who know us better than we would like to believe. If we have the reputation of being someone who prefers to shrug off early alarms, false or legitimate, our competitors will use that intel to their advantage. I'm reminded of the classic 1966 movie *How to Steal a Million*, with Peter O'Toole and Audrey Hepburn. In this film, the objective of the caper was to steal a forgery from a Paris museum, so that the forger wouldn't be caught and thrown into prison. The task was to turn off the protective laser beams that surrounded the statue on its plinth. The art thief made the night security guards *themselves* turn off the beams. How? By introducing false alarms, of course. Hiding in a janitor's closet, he popped out just long enough to throw what the screenwriter called a *boomerang* (but we Aussies know better; it wasn't).

The weapon would fly around the statue and break the laser beams before returning to the thief's hands, setting off the alarm bells. The head security guard would emerge from his cozy office (and card game and wine) and soon an added flurry of police would find nothing amiss and reset the alarm. He would then return to his colleagues and the game.

And the thief did it again. Setting off the alarm and returning to his hiding place with weapon in hand, ready to deploy one more time if necessary.

It only happened twice before the exasperated guard simply turned off the alarm system altogether. The call of his own personal comfort zone was stronger than his need to be on the alert. By morning, there was nothing left of the exhibit but an empty plinth, with an empty wine bottle replacing the statue.

"That's just a movie. That could never happen to me," you might say—maybe giving in to your own normalcy bias? Just a little bit?

Ask the man who still cringes at the memories of a cold, wet, rainy sidewalk one November night in London.

BEST: Resolve to pay attention to all alarm bells, no matter what you secretly might think of them.

WORST: Get too comfortable in the safe embrace of familiarity.

FIRST: Take action at the sound of the first alarm.

Chapter 18

"ARE YOU OKAY?" MEANS "ARE *WE* OKAY?"

I t was during the 2008–2009 financial crisis when it dawned on me: Leaders can send out expertly crafted messaging through emails, video appearances, speeches, and press releases until they're blue in the face. You might have all the words pitch-perfect. You might be a master at persuasive presentations on camera. You might deftly handle the toughest questions coming from the CNBC analysts and experts, cleverly slipping out of the hooks of a loaded question that might have otherwise caused your stock price to come crashing down.

But all those clever skills and stagecraft will come to nothing if you overlook—or underestimate—this one detail that distracted leaders are likely to miss: Your tribe members are already actively involved—*affected* might be the better word—by the headlines and your company's responses to the current circumstances, for better or for worse. And they want to play a part in saving their company so that it will thrive well into the future. And to do so requires them to notice all the signals they can. The look on your face is one of the first signals they'll pick up on.

Your tribe members are watching you. Very carefully. The words coming out of your mouth must match the look in your eye in an unguarded moment when you think no one can see you. There is never an unguarded moment when you're the leader. As Marshall Goldsmith says before stepping onto a stage for a speech, "It's showtime!" When you're the leader, showtime is all the time.

The message of your show? A consistent reminder that "*We* is not just me. *We* is all of us. In this together."

I discovered in a whole new way the power of the tribal *us*, more powerful than the *you* or *I*.

If you don't remember the 2008–2009 financial crisis, here is a brief overview of the suffering that it caused: In the United States alone, roughly 8.7 million jobs were lost between December 2007 and early 2010. Unemployment rates hit 10% in October 2009. Business bankruptcy filings rose from 28,322 in 2007 to 43,546 in 2008 and 60,837 in 2009. And people lost their homes at devastating rates. Foreclosure filings rose 120% from 2007 to 2009 with a record 2.8 million properties. Americans lost over $19 trillion in net worth during this period.

Every global crisis, the pandemic of 2020 being a more recent example, has an oppressive feeling of contagion. It hovers over the people you care for and who you depend on to keep their confidence in a future that's more positive than their present reality. Even if you weren't directly impacted by a bankruptcy or foreclosure, you very likely knew someone who was. You can practically see the thoughts hanging over their heads like hatchets on fraying ropes: "How will this current situation affect me?" "Will I catch the misfortune?" "My spouse has just been laid off. How will we manage on one income?"

"How can I be so sure that this company will survive the very thing that has destroyed so many other companies—the larger, more established, more successful ones?" "Is the CEO up to the task of piloting us through this choppy water?"

"Is he okay?" "Are we okay?" "Am *I* okay?"

There was only one way for us at WD-40 Company to find out: to navigate ourselves *through* this time of existential uncertainty. There was certainly no getting around it. This crisis was a global one. WD-40 Company was a global company. There was no metaphorical island anywhere with a safe side for us to ride out this hurricane. We were our own hurricane harbor. We took the position of, "We're going to ride this out together. And we're going to start by having some very clear objectives."

The number one objective was the caring and the well-being of our people. When we started off on the journey, I began to notice that people were increasingly interested in my own personal well-being. As I traveled around the world, and walked around our various company locations, I noticed that there was both earnestness and accelerating frequency in the question: "Garry, are you okay?"

And I would answer, "Yeah, I'm okay." And then think nothing of it. Until a few minutes later when the question was asked again by someone else. I initially assumed that they were asking whether the situation was overburdening me. But I soon realized that they were seeking an assurance that *they* were okay. That the company was basically okay. That they were still protected by a company that prioritized their well-being.

I realized that if I wasn't able to authentically project the confidence that this is not the end of the world and that we would indeed be okay in the future, then they were not okay right now. That's what they really wanted to know. Our job as leaders, again, was to communicate a *realistic* confidence—backed up by confident behaviors—that we were going to get through this. The people we have the privilege to lead are looking at us much more intently than they would when things are going swimmingly. Now they see that their abilities to survive their own present situation are linked to what we are *all* doing as leaders and as fellow tribe members. They need to trust their faith in their tribe. And they need to play an active role themselves in doing what it takes to take the company, themselves, and each other into a future that ignites their aspirations.

I discovered that once our objectives and priorities were clearly identified and communicated, we had to bring our tribe into the mission of saving the day. We had to give them an active role in discovering and implementing the solutions. Some elements of crisis management, of course, could only be handled in the boardroom or behind C-suite doors. But that didn't mean our people were powerless to make a difference. Since we are literally all in this together, why not bring all of us into the job of activating meaningful solutions? Even the seemingly most insignificant ones? It's never any good for us to say, "Everything's okay. Just trust us leaders to get us through this. You just go back to what you were doing."

At WD-40 Company, we were all taking important mitigation steps, some seemingly trivial. For example, we quickly realized we didn't need five subscriptions to the *Wall Street Journal*. We could get one, and people could share it around in the office if they wanted to. So we saved maybe $1,000 on those extra subscriptions. So what? How could that possibly help us survive a world on fire?

This small, seemingly insignificant step inspired a campaign of looking for more opportunities for the entire tribe to secure the business in this very uncertain time. This is when we launched new initiatives that pulled us all together. Some might call them cuts. I would call them *changes in behaviors*. For instance, we instigated the Stupid Policies Program. We engaged our entire global tribe with this challenge: "Let's look at everything we do. What policies or procedures do we have in place that are stupid and not adding value? Now is our time to reevaluate everything."

We were very, very deliberate about really understanding what mattered, which was taking care of our people, serving our customers, and being flexible. The Stupid Policies campaign became our magnifying glass that identified things that allowed us to conclude, "Well, we shouldn't do that anymore. Or maybe we should do this." We were forced to focus on what really mattered, and it caused us to be comfortable with doing things that would have been uncomfortable at other times.

One by one, department by department, country by country, people stepped up and said, "This policy isn't adding value." Or "This policy is creating more administrative burden than any value that it's delivering." We discovered that there were two real categories of stupid policies. The first is what we had expected: The policy was stupid. Or the procedure was stupid. And we just hadn't taken the time to realize it in the past. The second category was the legitimate policies that people had started to believe were stupid. This category told us that we had done a very poor job of communicating the value that a particular policy was delivering. So this gave us the opportunity to revisit all policies and identify which ones needed recommunicating, and which ones needed jettisoning altogether.

This is just one example of the many initiatives we put into place to ride out this particular hurricane, while keeping our cultural promise to our people—and consequently their faith in us—intact. Those were two very hard years, not to mention the months leading up to them and the months following. But we pulled through as a tribe and emerged out the other side with our objective of putting the well-being of our people first proven and protected. In an era when millions of people lost their jobs through layoffs and closures, everyone showed up at work even stronger as a tribe. During my entire tenure at the helm of WD-40 Company, not one person was laid off.

We implemented a hiring freeze. Not only did we want to avoid bringing new tribe members onboard during a time when the sustainability of such a decision was uncertain, but we were also acutely aware that every new hire might have left a relatively secure position to join us. We didn't want to encourage anyone to take that risk in their own careers and well-being. No one received raises or bonuses. Only extremely essential travel was allowed. A year or two earlier we had restructured our compensation plan to better serve both tribe members and shareholders. And it was proving itself to be a solid plan during these difficult times.

We lived by the philosophy that it was better that all of us suffered a little than that a few suffered a lot. Even these decisions demonstrated that we were confident we would be okay. More than okay, actually. We knew that these sacrifices and mitigations would certainly pay off one day with a stronger company and a resilient tribe. We had faith in a future that was worth the sacrifices we shouldered at the moment.

Ken Blanchard says, "None of us is as good as all of us." The financial crisis proved that to be truer than, perhaps, even he knew. The invitation for all of us to band together in the tribal spirit and contribute our best to the shared mission may have begun with each WD-40 Company tribe member secretly glancing at my face and watching how the way I acted matched what I was saying.

The way I looked and behaved signaled to them that if we all banded together, we could see our way through this crisis. Gradually the question "Are *you* okay?" morphed into "What more can *we* do as a tribe to see us through this?"

BEST: Always include every tribe member in the shared objective of successfully achieving company goals, no matter the external circumstances.

WORST: Hide the truth from your people. This includes lying about the facts or faking your faith in the company. It also includes making yourself inaccessible to your tribe members—emotionally and physically. If you're inaccessible to them, they are also inaccessible to you.

FIRST: Dedicate yourself to the belief that empowering your people to take active roles in surviving any crisis before you will multiply the odds of prevailing over even the worst of circumstances.

Chapter 19

TIMELESS WISDOM COMES FROM UNCERTAIN TIMES

I t was the first week of March 2024. As we were developing the first draft of the manuscript that would eventually become this book, Facebook and LinkedIn were crowded with memes all proclaiming various versions of this one inescapable fact:

> Four years ago this week, we were living our last week of normalcy. Four years ago next week, things would never be the same again. But we didn't know it yet.

Do you remember where you were and what you were doing on March 5, 2020? Living a normal life with maybe just one ear cocked to the news? You might not remember any of the details from that day. Why? Because it was so, well, normal. Consequently, forgettable.

Around the world, business travelers would point to Friday the 13th, when hundreds of thousands of road warriors were rushing to airports in order to get home before it would become too complicated to get there. Or maybe even impossible. A few days later, a global lockdown commenced. And our collective memory of the following months and years is filled with images of Zoom calls; the daily banging of pots and pans to announce the end of shifts of exhausted health care workers; hands of young loved ones reaching out to their aging, isolated grandparents through impenetrable window glass. I don't have to tell you. You remember it all.

As for me, things began to change a couple of weeks beforehand. It was late February. I was, as usual, traveling. I was in Palermo, Italy, on my way to a conference for my company. At this point, we already knew that China was reporting devastating illness and deaths. During that time, Italy got hit with the pandemic. One by one, meetings all over the planet were canceled. The effects of this mysterious and deadly contagion rolled around the globe like that big stone ball in the movie *Raiders of the Lost Ark*. I felt like Indiana Jones, running just barely ahead of it, working with our leaders to ensure all our facilities across 15 countries had action plans in place. I also needed to get safely back to California in time to walk through my own front door and close it behind me by the time the calendar flipped to March 16.

At that point, the entire world community entered a chapter in the history of humanity that none of us had ever experienced at such an epic scale, with an outcome that we haven't yet completely grasped four years later. We're still feeling the ripple effects. In politics. In public health policy. In our relationships with family and friends. In weakened trust in institutions that we had always counted on for our safety and well-being.

In those early days, I couldn't know the full extent of the upheaval in civilization, of course. Just like everyone else, I was just another bloke trying to figure it out as I went. But I held one consideration above all else as I tried to discern what each next right step would be. And that was this:

The well-being of our people came first. Period.

Now four years later, as I look back on what I've learned, a handful of very simple lessons rise to the surface. As I often say, they're simple. But they're not easy. And, in their implementation, they may look different to you in your experience than they do to me in my experience. But let's give it a go anyway.

Don't try to seize control of a fluid situation by making premature pronouncements. When we're in the middle of a swirling tornado of chaos, it's natural for us to want to seize at least one stable point of certainty. The hope is that at least other swirling elements in its orbit might settle down—or at least slow down. That drive to declare control over something, *anything*, is heightened by the pressure of our people looking to us, crying, "What do we do? What do we do?" We're seeing the cost of many leaders giving in to that natural impulse today as companies increasingly roll back their remote working policy that they installed when it looked as though daily office life might be a thing of the past forever. Hundreds of thousands of valuable employees jumped at the opportunity to move their families far away from their place of employment—to a destination where the cost of living was less, crime was lower, schools were better, the fishing was good. Whatever the reason, they were thrilled to relocate. But now, as I write this in 2024, employers are beginning to claw back that policy and call everyone back to their office. Families everywhere are being split up because the major breadwinner must resume their commute back to headquarters, this time cross-country, by air. The economic and emotional price they're paying for a precipitous policy change made in a time of crisis will have negative impacts deep into the future.

All a leader has to do when being pressured to make a decision *now now now* is simply say, "I don't know yet. Let's give it more time and see. In the meantime, here is the temporary plan." At WD-40 Company, our interim plan was a policy that we called "work from where," which essentially meant "work from anywhere." As locations began to slowly open up, and offices began to slowly turn their lights back on, we continued to leave it up to our tribe members to do the right thing. Our number one value.

Keep a light touch on the controls. If you ever have the chance to watch Col. Nicole Malachowski (USAF, retired), the first female fighter pilot in the Thunderbirds, talk about what it's like to fly in such breathtakingly tight and fast formations, don't miss it. She inspires the principle to "fly loose," advising us leaders to resist the urge to micromanage when conditions start getting, shall we say, "off plan." In her training and now her speeches, she points out that when flying in tight formations at a respectable speed of 500 miles an hour, wingtip to wingtip, there's no room for improvisation. Each pilot is expected to fly exactly according to plan with a light touch on the controls. Any rogue reaction by one pilot to an impulsive behavior of another pilot becomes an overreaction by all the pilots, which then produces what she calls "pilot-induced oscillation." And then, as she puts it in exquisite, tragic understatement, that makes for an "ugly" performance. Impressive, to be sure. And memorable. But in all the wrong ways.

After one board of directors meeting a few years ago, a board member remarked to me, "It's in tough times like this when character is really tested." I responded, "It's in tough times like this when *our culture* is really tested." Part of our culture is the "fly loose" philosophy. To have in place the plan, the responses to predictable contingencies, where we have a light touch on the controls, we're watching what's going on with full situational awareness, and trusting our tribe members to stay the course faithful and loyal to the strategy.

It's fashionable these days to speak of resilience, especially in the context of rebounding from hard times and hard knocks. But I think that resilience starts with adherence: our adherence to the promises we make to ourselves and each other when everyone is safely on the ground. That way, when things start getting really real, so will be our promise to fly together. Wingtip to wingtip. Just as planned.

Don't make new decisions based on old objectives, beliefs, and variables. I must confess something. When we were forced into lockdown—and working from home was not a choice, it was a mandate—I did worry about the possibility of our productivity plummeting. I had a belief—one that I would have been a little ashamed of had I been fully aware of it—that people had to be physically present in order to be productive. In this new work-from-home scenario, I immediately imagined a lot of poolside languishing, the slathering on of sunscreen, and not much getting done in the way of WD-40 Company goals and objectives. Come to find out, sunscreen and WD-40 did mix quite nicely. Yes, there were pools in the background of our Zoom meetings. And yes, indeed, all the work was being done.

Come to find out that my belief that desk presence was an essential ingredient to company and culture was either outdated or simply flat-out wrong. In my reluctance to fully have faith in my tribe members to perform on their own, without the supervision that comes with being at their workstations, I was actually pursuing the wrong thing: the need for control, not the ideal of unleashing them to do their very best work in a setting where they were most comfortable and felt the safest at the time.

Because of the government-mandated shutdown, I was forced to give up this level of control that I didn't even know I was valuing. Because I try to keep my eyes and mind open most of the time, and practice self-awareness at every opportunity, I discovered that I had been chasing the wrong thing: the illusion of control rather than the productivity itself.

I assume you have read or at least heard about the book *Who Moved My Cheese?*. It's a fable of four mice in search of food that isn't where they were used to finding it. In the sequel, *Out of the Maze: An A-Mazing Way to Get Unstuck*, one of the characters, Hem, continues his adventures in search of cheese. Along the way, he discovers apples. Even though they are more delicious than the cheese he is pursuing, he dismisses the apples because they're not what he thought he wanted. He wanted nourishment and he was operating on the limiting belief that that nourishment was available only through cheese. So, nuts to the apples, right? As the story ends, Hem learns to love apples. And gathers a few lessons along the way. Here is a sampling:

- "Notice your beliefs: A belief is a thought that you trust to be true."
- "Don't believe everything you think: Sometimes 'facts' are just how you see things."
- "Let go of what isn't working: You can't launch a new quest with old baggage."

- "Choose a new belief: Changing what you think doesn't change who you are."

Recognize that your people are on a hero's journey of their own.
The character Hem is on a classic hero's journey, setting out on a quest and transforming into a better version of himself along the way. Everyone, in certain or uncertain times, whether they know it or not, like it or not, is also on a hero's journey. Life is an adventure, even when day after day it feels so repetitive it's like the movie *Groundhog Day*. Something is bound to come up eventually for all of us and shake all the bits, drop us square on our bum, and challenge us to rise back up to our feet better people for having had the experience.

In uncertain times, that journey becomes even more harrowing. Our tribe members suffer great personal losses and the tragedies of loved ones' deaths. The freeze/flight/flee reactions to squaring off face-to-face with a fear, or in the case of uncertain times, multiple fears barreling toward them all at once. Each life-changing misadventure doesn't politely wait for its predecessor to complete its mayhem before stepping up to the plate for its own turn at the bat.

It's a clown car of catastrophes that we must deal with in uncertain times.

As leaders, we must remember that our people have had to envision, prepare for, endure, and then recover from worst-case scenarios. They've learned new ways of managing their panic, new ways of facing fear head-on, new ways of finding the gifts in the midst of terror and disaster.

Will they tell you about it? Maybe. Or maybe not. They'll show up at work. Take their seat at the meeting table. Offer you coffee as they pour a cup of their own. Laugh at appropriate times. But the signs of a deepening transformation are there if you look carefully. Usually just around the eyes.

BEST: Embrace the Learning Moment. Uncertain times are the perfect environment for proving to your people that you stand by the Learning Moment philosophy. As they take risks in an extraordinarily harrowing time, now's your chance to prove that you stand by keeping the Learning Moment idea safe and welcome in your workplace.

WORST: Give in to your own fears within earshot of people who are depending on you for being that source of stability. Never lie to your people, of course. But if you know that you're prone to alarming emotional outbursts as a way of releasing pent-up stress and tension, take it outside, as they say.

FIRST: When facing an oncoming crisis, stop and remind yourself exactly whose needs and well-being you are primarily responsible for. What constituency comes in second. Which one comes in third.

Chapter 20

YOUR WORKPLACE CAN BE YOUR TRIBE'S RECOMBOBULATION ZONE

When we think about workplace culture, it can be tempting to think of the individual's experience inside that culture as just that—*inside* the metaphorical walls of the workplace experience itself. We imagine the day-to-day interactions of our tribe members working and thriving together, developing, achieving all the goals that make our businesses hum. Caring for and protecting each other. Even though we leaders are likely aware that everyone has a personal life, are we really fully cognizant of the fact that every single one of us is on a heroic journey of our own? A transformative, challenging, harrowing adventure that runs parallel to the business's main plot of enterprising success?

Depending on the nature of each personal heroic journey, it's very likely that, for many, your workplace environment is actually a place of refuge from the major life stresses your people are facing outside of work. The workplace culture is a place where they can take a breather from their personal chaos, find solace in the company of others, gather their wits in an environment that's relatively predictable. It can be your tribe's *recombobulation area*—a wonderful concept I picked up while flying out of Milwaukee's Mitchell International Airport one day.

While the business of aviation and airport management continues to operate according to process and strategy, each passenger is living out a personal heroic journey that requires air travel. Running parallel to all the moving parts required to sustain a profitable and dependable aviation industry are millions of personal dramas that all converge at security.

Picture this: You're going through security. Shoes are off. Belt's off. Loose change is in a pile in the gray bin by your very expensive laptop. Your wallet is somewhere—you just saw it a second ago. The passenger behind you is breathing down your neck. The passenger in front of you won't hurry up, for Pete's sake.

You're surrounded by commands. Stop! Go! Arms up. Feet apart! Turn around! No joking. Go back and do it again! Don't touch that! Step aside! Not there! Stand here! Don't just stand there. Move! Move! Move!

Mayhem threatens to overwhelm you. Once you get past that chaos, all you want is a quiet place to gather your wits and your belongings. In Milwaukee, that would be the recombobulation area.

This is where you can take a moment. Reorient yourself. And just breathe.

Who can't smile at the sound of *recombobulation*? Who can't relate? Maybe even smile at the gentle lightheartedness of the word.

The concept of *recombobulation* offers that feeling of safety, of well-being, of being taken care of. A space set aside—either a physical space, emotional space, or cultural space—where you can safely attend to your own needs without holding up the many other things going on around you.

A place where caring souls can watch over you, maybe subtly, maybe overtly. Maybe just to ask, "Hey, are you okay?" At work, that feeling isn't just restricted to a single room. It can permeate your entire environment.

If that experience is created, fostered, and encouraged by leadership, so much the better. Then it becomes an integral part of your culture, one in which everyone owns the just cause of supporting each other's needs for achieving well-being, while taking care of the enterprise. It's not an either/or choice. It's a scenario that's *mutually essential*. As we've discussed earlier in this book, in my earliest days I chose the Indigenous culture of my native Australia as the inspiration for a tribal feeling I thought would best move us all toward the business future that matched our vision.

I defined *tribe* as "a group of people who come together to protect and feed one another."

As the years progressed, I discovered more layers to the concept of workplace tribe that extend far beyond the physical business environment and into each other's personal lives. Running parallel to the epic story of the enterprise itself are hundreds, even thousands, of individual heroic journeys of all the people in your care. Each person comes to work with the business objectives of the day mapped out, but also with an entirely different life adventure unfolding—fears, goals, failures, accomplishments, tragedies, hopes, dreams, losses, joys.

The workplace, alongside their colleagues, is a place apart where they can marshal their resources, get the help they need, and rest their hearts and minds in the company of people who sincerely care about them. It can be their recombobulation area.

Nothing drives that point home more poignantly than when a tribe member is hit with a cancer diagnosis. I wish I could take personal credit for what happened next when a young couple who both worked at WD-40 Company went to the HR department to address the business side of the most devastating news two young parents could face: their child had leukemia. But then again, I'm glad I can't. Because everyone else in the tribe kicked into immediate action. No one needed my permission. And they knew it.

Word got out. Not in a privacy violation way. But in an all-hands-on-deck kind of way. The grapevine hummed. Plans were laid. HR set up a PTO donation program, and quickly this young mother and father had all the time off they would need to do nothing but focus on what was most important—the health and well-being of their little girl. The tribe surrounded them, lifted them up, protected them, and, yes, fed them. And celebrated with them when the happy outcome was announced. They recombobulated. The young family and the entire tribe alike.

This tribal encircling is possible in any workplace culture where leaders are committed to the happiness of their people. It takes focus and intention. But it's not an unnatural stretch to achieve a culture where people just kick into gear because, of course, it's the right thing to do.

Remember the concept of PERMA in chapter 14? People flourish when they have positive emotions, engagement, relationships that are emotionally healthy, meaning in life, and a sense of accomplishment.

As natural as these components may be, the leaders must care enough to make sure they're in place and nurtured through good times and bad. Even your demonstrated commitment to your people's well-being is, in and of itself, a recombobulation area.

In January of 2021, when we were still in the throes of Covid dread and uncertainty, we decided to administer a special pulse survey to see how everyone was coping. We had just conducted the regularly scheduled survey before Covid changed all our lives. Because we stayed true to WD-40 Company's values, even in such a time of true uncertainty, I had expected the numbers to be relatively the same. Which, of course, turned out to be the case.

Except one item on the survey, which actually went up. It was the question, "I'm excited about my place in the company's future." Well, that was surprising. Everyone was home, isolated, alone with their own thoughts—nothing about the future glimmered with hope at that particular moment. And yet, everyone was excited about their place in the company's future. So I explored further. And this is what I was told:

"I feel safe."

We as a company were doing our best to live out our promise of taking care of our people. We were holding informal Zoom meetings where tribe members all over the world could gather over mealtime and just relax together. We had coffee chats. We brought in experts to talk to us about anxiety. We even had a comedian perform an online show that featured magic tricks that awed even the most skeptical among us.

We, in short, kept it together. We kept us together. Reassured. Safe.

Isn't that what the recombobulation area is all about?

BEST: Bear in mind that, for many of your people, the workplace is a refuge from the chaos of everyday life.

WORST: Be so focused on deliverables and deadlines that you overlook the fact that each of your people are dealing with pressures that might not be visible at work.

FIRST: Resolve to make the care of your people your foremost priority, especially in days of upheaval and uncertainty.

Chapter 21

CANDOR IS THE CORNERSTONE OF TRUST IN UNCERTAIN TIMES

When in doubt, get real. I know, that's easy to say. But not exactly easy to do when circumstances all around you are happening so fast, moving in so many different directions, demanding so much of your attention this way and that. These are the conditions when it's most essential to remember what your principles and values are. But, ironically, these are also the conditions when principles and values are the first to fly out the window. You are stuck in reactive mode. And you're too busy and distracted to even recognize that much. Pay close attention, if you can, during these times. This is when the aha moments come at you fast.

Here's how it happened to me . . .

Over the years I have grown very fond of this one particular MO: "No lying, no faking, no hiding." Seems reasonable enough. No leader likes to be lied to. A fudged deadline. An erased (or added) line on an expense report. Finessed RFPs where favored contractors win the business in a succession of no-bid scenarios. A crucial detail left out of an annual report or call with investors. Any number of day-to-day details could be the catalyst to catastrophic losses or court cases where the odds aren't in the company's favor. No. It's much better that we're all on the up-and-up. And that we make sure the rest of the tribe knows that's what's expected.

A tribal culture where it's safe to tell the truth may not necessarily be the easiest place to work every day. But at least your people know what's at stake for them by telling the truth. And are counted on by their tribe members and coaches to be consistently trustworthy. I can't think of a single leader who would disagree with me on this point. In fact, you may be wondering, "Garry, why are you making me read this obvious lesson?"

Ah. Glad you asked.

How would it be if the tables were turned and *you* were on the hot seat for telling an uncomfortable truth?

Oh, you think. *Well, that depends on the situation.* No. It. Doesn't.

At WD-40 Company, we had a specially designated room where truths were exchanged and ideas were born. Initially, our idea was to call it the War Room, which paired nicely with our other concept, the Peace Room, a serene library. After some thought, though, I realized that I really didn't like the word *war* attached to a space specially designated for uncomfortable conversations.

Might as well install a blood pressure cuff in its own special cubby right by the door. Can you imagine how that would go? Picture for a moment that you've been summoned. "Please meet me in the War Room at 2 PM this afternoon." You are greeted by an attendant with these words: "Here, put your cell phone in this basket, and roll up your sleeve, please. Just relax, now. This might get a little tight but just for a minute. It won't hurt. Hmmmmm. When was the last time you saw your doctor?"

No. That clearly wasn't going to work. So we named that room the Cave instead. Still, there was no escaping the fact that any invitation to the Cave would be the first hint that someone would soon be engaging in a meaningful conversation; it might even be a little uncomfortable.

The truth must be told. Which is hard enough on the recipient of the truth. But how about the messenger? I had truly underestimated how difficult it would be to speak the truth when I suspected that the truth would wreck the recipient's day, if not week, or entire career.

So I agonized over the prospect of having one of those conversations. Here I was, Mr. No Lying, Hiding, Faking. But in pursuit of my own comfort zone, that's exactly what I wanted to do. Lie (by omission), hide (definitely), fake (very much, most definitely). Couldn't time simply take care of things on its own? What if I handle a situation all wrong and destroy our relationship?

Then I remembered the words of Ron Carucci, author of the book *To Be Honest: Lead with the Power of Truth, Justice and Purpose*:

> The more uncomfortable the prospect of telling the truth might be, the more essential and valuable it is likely to be to both the messenger and the recipient of that message. Leaders who choose to hide the truth for the sake of staying in their own comfort zone deny themselves the rich opportunity to help someone else on their own career or life journey.

So there I was having a moment of uncomfortable truth telling...with myself. Which, truth be told, wasn't the most comfortable conversation I had ever had with myself either. But it must be done. Reflecting back on Ron's words, I reassured myself that I wasn't the first person who struggled with this responsibility. Otherwise, he wouldn't have had to say this.

So then I thought:

If I really do love my people, I should be brave enough to be able to share opportunities for them to redirect themselves, their behavior, or their output to achieve better outcomes. Why am I feeling so, so afraid of doing this? I love this person and want him to be successful.

And maybe I was the one who needed the redirection. In my efforts to protect him from the negative feelings that sometimes can come with coaching (especially in the Cave), I had been unclear about what my expectations are. As a result, this person had every right to give me some truth: I had not been clear what I had really wanted in his performance. We let people down when we're not clear on what we expect from each other.

I concluded with this self-assessment: "You're a dumb-ass, Garry."

With that, I stepped into the Cave to have the truthful conversation with my tribe member, who, in the safe context of our mutually respectful relationship, had the confidence he needed to hear the truth that would help him meet our agreed-upon, and very clear, expectations. In the context of mutual respect. And trust.

Carucci once told me, "We're in a trust recession these days. And it's getting worse because people are making up ways to manage their uncertainty, instead of having candid, honest conversations with each other. And then things just become more uncertain.

"When your actions and words don't match, you're three times more likely to have people lie. You've now told people, 'It's perfectly okay around here to say one thing and do another.' Which they then will."

Still, that comfort zone calls to you: "Wouldn't you rather come sit by me?" Why, yes, you would. But your preference isn't what counts here. In our role as leaders, this means that our primary responsibility in every interaction with our people is to help them be better at the work they do. Being a leader isn't about inflating our egos or exerting some kind of dominance. It's about entering into the coaching conversations with an honest heart, even though the circumstances might require a certain amount of toughness. It's a balance between being candid (tough-minded) and caring (tenderhearted).

I'd like to think I always lead with a tender heart, or at least a balanced position. But in all candor, I can easily go the other way if I'm not careful. I have enough self-awareness to know it, and enough humility to admit it (although that second part isn't as easy as the first). But when I let my ego take over and allow my value of candor to unintentionally diminish caring, people experience a behavior that they don't deserve. So, just to stay in my comfort zone, I have the tendency to overcompensate. Which doesn't help anyone.

I have to watch myself every day. Because of my own caring for my tribe, I can very easily stray into the tenderhearted realm, where I become soft to the point that I'm no longer helping the person I'm coaching. I become overly compassionate, losing sight of my duty to help that tribe member achieve the best outcome for all of us.

Whether your nature is to reside on the tenderhearted end of the caring continuum or on the tough end, you're abdicating your responsibility as a leader. Neither end is effective in our coaching communications.

But you are human too. And you deserve and require the emotional support necessary to meet your leadership role. This is something you need to hear on a regular basis from someone who cares enough about you to be honest.

BEST: Always be aware of the power of your leadership position. No matter how wounded, betrayed, or cheated you may be feeling at the time, the wrong word from you, delivered in a thoughtless, emotional way, could devastate your tribe member.

WORST: Assume you can read people's minds or that they should read yours. I wonder how many valuable relationships are ruined because of misunderstandings that could have been easily straightened out with just a handful of calm, exploratory questions.

FIRST: Always start out by assuming positive intent. In most cases, people don't come to work with the intention of destroying their company or compromising an initiative they're working on. They are not likely to be saboteurs. They're just people doing their best. And screwing up now and then. So are you. Now there's something you two have in common.

CHEERS, MATE!

Chapter 22

WILL YOU BE BETTER TOMORROW THAN YOU ARE TODAY?

So tell me, where do you expect to see yourself in five years?"

How many job interviews have you been on where you've been asked that question? How many job interviews have you conducted where you have asked that question of candidates yourself?

The first people who inserted that question into their interview scripts probably thought they knew what they were doing. Such a smart question, they might have thought, calibrated to discern the candidate's ambition, drive to succeed, clearly defined and articulated personal goals. One would hope. At the very least, it filled up about five minutes of the scheduled interview time, as each candidate would awkwardly fumble for what might be the answer most pleasing to the hiring manager's ears.

But more likely than not, the candidate's answer will only show you how carefully rehearsed the canned response had been the night before. In front of the spouse. In front of a mirror. In front of the dog. It didn't matter. The answer was queued up, teed up, ready to deploy. Would the question come before or after the other classic: "What's your greatest weakness?"

What does the answer tell the hiring manager? The candidate has been around this block before. How many times? The candidate is expressing aggressive ambition (possibly a good thing) without any full understanding that the dream scenario just described would require that the incumbent will have lost the job. (Possibly a bad thing . . . Where's the humanity? Where's the humility? Where's the spirit of servant leadership?) Or the candidate paints a picture of the company's values made manifest in some way, through the candidate's future dedication and effort. Okay. That just tells you the candidate studied the website last night. A good sign, but, still, is it the best indicator that candidate will fit into your tribe?

And, unhappily for the candidates, they have no idea how they're coming across when they try to answer that question with confidence, enthusiasm, and clarity. Maybe too aggressive? Maybe a little too *too*? Very likely inauthentic.

I've got a new question for you to throw into the mix:

"How are you better today than you were yesterday?"

How's that for a curveball? Unless the whole world reads this book, candidates are unlikely to have prepared for this question in advance. And even if they had, so much the better. Their answers will demonstrate their commitment to continuous learning and self-awareness. How bad could that be?

Which brings us back to you: Are continuous learning and growing self-awareness key components of *your* life?

How are you better today than you were yesterday?

If you're just starting out in your career, the acquisition of skill sets might be top of mind more than the development of interpersonal skills. It would be completely understandable and acceptable if you said, "Well, I just received my certificate of completion from that course on advanced Excel techniques. I'm pretty proud of that." And that's good.

But as you rise into the leadership ranks, wise hiring managers and coaches are going to want to know, "How are you a better *person* today than you were yesterday? How will you be a better person tomorrow than today?" In other words, "How are you with people? With self-awareness? With being coachable? With improving?"

You will (or at least should) always have something new to report. For instance, you're almost done with this book. What you have learned that might have changed you, even just the slightest bit? Have you put any of the learnings into practice already so that you can honestly say that you are on that continuous—even if sometimes disruptive—path of personal development?

Imagine you're sitting with your coach, who asks you, "How are you a better person today than you were yesterday?" What might be some of the developments that you have already pulled from this book and activated in your own life?

"The other day I learned about Learning Moments, and how both successes and failures can be experiences that will benefit my entire team. As long as we hold the belief that our people are safe— even celebrated—when describing a Learning Moment to benefit everyone. So today I'm a better leader by helping people trust that it's okay to share experiences with their teammates."

"The other day I read that the best way to coach someone is in private one-on-one conversations so that they will feel supported, not shamed in front of their colleagues. Yesterday I had the opportunity to have a sensitive conversation with a tribe member, where no one else could hear. It ended really well, with a lot of clarity between us. And today is the first day that I will *always* have those conversations in private."

"The other day I had this aha moment that our workplace can actually be a comforting source of mental health for a lot of us. No. For *all* of us. I never thought of work that way before. Yesterday one of our team members, who works remotely, sent us all an email sounding overwhelmed and demoralized. I remembered reading that connection is an essential component of mental health. So, after making sure it was okay first, I drove over to her house and we had an impromptu meeting right there in her living room. Today I am the kind of leader who looks for opportunities for all of us to get together, either virtually or in person, even if it's just to have an informal chat over coffee."

"I just read in the book *The Coaching Habit* that asking people *why* they do something risks making them feel defensive. Michael Bungay Stanier wrote that asking questions by starting out with *what* gets you the information you need in a psychologically safe setting. Today I'm a leader who is very careful about the way I speak to my team, even down to the way I phrase a risky question."

We can be continuous learners, but we all have to start somewhere. For me that journey to becoming a better person tomorrow than I am today started with my studies with Ken Blanchard at the

University of San Diego. That is where I wrote my first life purpose (an exercise that taught me a lot about the power of values). I still have it:

> My life purpose is to use my leadership skills and common sense to motivate and encourage people so they can maximize their opportunities, meet our common goals and have a lot of fun doing it. My paramount aim is to act in the best interest of those I lead.

I had come a long way from my childhood days in Five Dock, and my Beijing adventures of trying to foist oil samples on busy Chinese buyers who could get all the lubricant they wanted for free. Just over there in that big bucket. I had discovered that to be successful as a leader, I couldn't change people. I had to change myself. That's when I got really conscious about how I would behave to bring out the best of others.

This journey changes us as people, for the better, if we choose to put our heart into the effort. For instance, when I took the DISC profile (an assessment instrument that measures dominance, influence, steadiness, and conscientiousness), to no one's surprise, my results showed that I was on the extreme position of the D designation. This meant that my go-to style is: "Be brief, be bright, be gone." Which was fine for me but did nothing for people whose feelings I might hurt just by being my friendly self, however brief that interaction might be. It wasn't their job to bend around my nature. It was my responsibility to accommodate theirs.

At that time, I was working with a tribe member who I sincerely liked very much. But he drove me nuts. Where I was a D, he was an extreme I. This meant he was all about building relationships, even though, as far as I was concerned, we already had one. A good one. But my opinion wasn't what counted here. It was his need. So I developed a routine in advance of every meeting with him. It forced me to slow down and match *his* pace of interacting. Before going into his office, I would get a cup of coffee. And then I would tell myself, "I don't have to achieve anything in this meeting until I've drunk this coffee."

I let my coffee be my guide, and until I saw the bottom of the cup, it was in charge of my timing. And so we sat together. And talked. And built our relationship. He had the opportunity to be his great self with me. And I was still achieving what I needed to accomplish. First the task at hand. But most importantly, the development of rapport with a valued tribe member who knew he belonged. And he mattered to me.

As we begin our careers as leaders, we discover very quickly—assuming we're open to getting some tough news—that we have to focus on getting better and better at interpersonal behaviors and relationship skills. As Marshall Goldsmith says about leaders in his book *What Got You Here Won't Get You There*, what successful people might perceive to be strengths, others might experience as, well, *really* annoying. Even to the point of getting in the way of success: the company's success, their colleagues' success, and, of course, their own future prospects. He gives these examples:

- They think they have all the answers, but others see it as arrogance.
- They think they're contributing to a situation with helpful comments, but others see it as butting in.
- They think they're delegating effectively, but others see it as shirking responsibilities.

- They think they're holding their tongue, but others see it as unresponsiveness.
- They think they're letting people think for themselves, but others see it as ignoring them ...

Thanks to Marshall's influence, my learning never stops. The goal is always to be a better person today than I was yesterday. With his urging, I have a list of my own preferred behaviors and characteristics posted over my computer, under the heading: "Am I being the person I want to be right now?" I only have to look at the list to see that, yes, I still have some learning to do. Every. Single. Day. The list is a long one:

I want to be grateful.
I want to be caring.
I want to be empathetic.
I want to be reasonable.
I want to be a listener.
I want to be fact-based.
I want to have a balanced opinion.
I want to be curious.
I want to be a learner.
I want to throw sunshine, not shadow.

It's up to me to continuously learn how to be those things. That's the fun part. And the privilege. Not always pleasant. And I don't always come out of the experience without a scar or two. But that's when I resolve to learn some more.

Tomorrow I'll be even better for the effort. I hope.

BEST: Enjoy discovering those areas in life where learning more will help you be a better leader.

WORST: Assume that you can't learn from people in different positions on the org chart.

FIRST: Make a detailed list of how you want to improve in order to serve your people better. And then seek out the experts and coaches who will help you close those gaps.

Chapter 23

LEADERSHIP IS PURPOSE, NOT POWER

In the previous chapter, I shared with you the personal purpose statement I wrote in 2001. So you don't have to flip back to where you first read it, here it is again:

My life purpose is to use my leadership skills and common sense to motivate and encourage people so they can maximize their opportunities, meet our common goals and have a lot of fun doing it. My paramount aim is to act in the best interest of those I lead.

Now here's my current personal purpose statement:

I help leaders build cultures of belonging where love, forgiveness, and learning inspire a happier, more connected world.

There were quite a few iterations between 2001 and now. Each one reflecting my own stepping forward out of a yesterday version of what I thought a leader should be and into a more current version.

Step by step, refinement by refinement. Learning Moment after Learning Moment. And now here we are. Is this my last version? Only time will tell. (It goes without saying, though, that I hope you have already outgrown whatever personal purpose statement you might have had before you picked up this book. Back to the drawing board with you!)

If you were to stop me along my headlong, rushing way into the future and ask me about leadership, its power and purpose, I might have given you some well-intentioned, half-assed answer. Which was the best I could have done because I was learning along the way myself. But I think the main aha that has framed up all my learning along the way is this:

Leadership is a followership.

As a team, you're working together to face down an "enemy." In normal days, that enemy is the natural resistance that comes with reaching for a gigantic goal as a tribe. The fear. The self-doubt. The challenge to keep trusting each other, even through dramas that might arise. In abnormal times, that enemy might appear to be more overpowering. A global pandemic? A sudden economic downturn? Earthquakes? Political upheaval and the social divisiveness that comes along with it? You name it.

If you're a leader, whatever the biggest challenge is, it's not likely to be on your bingo card. Unpredictability. Unforeseen circumstances. It's what you signed up for. Did your tribe sign up for it too? Not really. They signed up for you, with the full faith and confidence that the tribe you have cultivated will see everyone through to better days beyond the immediate crisis.

If you're going to start marching toward the enemy, whatever it might be, do you have to call for your people to organize themselves, refocus, shake off the inertia, gather up their energy, and drive for the extra push?

Or are they already right there, with the words "We got your back!" on their lips? Which scenario appeals to you the most? I know which one I prefer.

How we create those followerships is not what happens on heroic days. It's what happens in the ordinary, in-between times, those interactions when you think a moment doesn't matter. That's when your behaviors count the most.

In chapter 16, I introduced you to Alec (or it could be Alice), the Soul-Sucking CEO, the leader people love to loathe. So who is the opposite of Alec? Let me introduce you to Susan (or could be Sam), otherwise known as Servant Leader. What do the Susans/Sams of the world do that the Alecs of the world overlook or even actively dismiss? Here's a short list to give you a running start in understanding all the approaches to leadership that are inspired by purpose instead of the personal ego rewards of power.

They:

Are constantly and consistently in servant leadership mode. We hear the expression *servant leadership* used so frequently these days that I wonder if it has lost its essential meaning. Who doesn't want to be known as a servant leader, right? No one is going to say, "I'm a command-and-control leader. It's my way or the highway."

Are you prepared to take on the personal sacrifices required to be a true servant leader? Are you willing to put your people first? To share information freely, promptly, and openly (where appropriate, of course)? To step out of the spotlight so that others are given the credit they deserve? When you're busy and preoccupied by a pressing situation, are you willing to set those thoughts aside to listen to your people with empathy and compassion? No matter how much time it takes?

Are competent in their own areas of expertise. Servant leaders rise through the ranks of their organization because of their original set of specialized skills, as well as their inclusive and inspiring leadership skills. They are trusted and respected for the contributions they bring to the tribe.

Are connected with their people. Servant leaders know what is going on with their tribe members, professionally and, where appropriate and welcome, personally. If their tribe is so large that they can't be involved one-on-one with everyone on a daily basis, they have intentionally set up a culture of freely expressed communication so that everyone can access their senior-most leaders—and each other—at will.

Love Learning Moments. Servant leaders intentionally create a psychologically safe cultural environment that encourages learning, experimentation, and innovation within the tribe. Tribe members are celebrated for sharing all kinds of Learning Moments, those with positive outcomes and those with disappointing results. They know that the freely shared Learning Moments today build healthy tribes equipped with the experiences and skills necessary to meet whatever the future throws at them.

Have a heart of gold and a backbone of steel. Servant leaders recognize that this is a tough balance to strike on the basis of day-to-day, moment-by-moment interactions. Develop a reputation for having a heart of gold and some might mistake you for being easily manipulated through emotional appeal. Develop a reputation for leading with only a backbone of steel, without any heart, and you will have fallen firmly in the command-and-control leadership category. Then you're an Alec, not a Sam. Develop a reputation for both, and you will serve a tribe through compassion, empathy, flexibility, standards, and boundaries into a successful future.

Are champions of hope. Servant leaders ignite sustainable inspiration among their tribe members by painting the future of their shared dreams in vivid, emotionally compelling detail. They connect the dots from their current situation to their desired condition, providing the training the tribe needs to reach each dot and proceed to their goal. When hit by unpredicted events that could otherwise sideline the tribe in discouragement, servant leaders signal through their own calm, resilient, flexible behaviors the message that the goal is still within reach.

Know that micromanagement isn't scalable. Just as servant leaders have their own areas of expertise and specialized skills, they recognize that their tribe members also have specialties that are likely beyond the reach of their leaders. Servant leaders know that giving their tribe members the autonomy they require and deserve to do their work as they see fit is the most efficient approach to moving the tribe as a community toward their future objectives. Micromanagement takes servant leaders away from their responsibilities and deprives their tribe members of the confidence-building opportunities to build up their respective expertise. It's when individual tribe members are fully equipped and experienced in their roles that they can then turn around and teach younger tribe members coming up behind them. Thereby building that essential talent and knowledge bank for the future.

Do what they say they're going to do. Servant leaders know that when they fulfill their commitments, they are actually fulfilling three responsibilities: accomplishing the task itself, demonstrating the standard of expected behaviors within the culture, and honoring the tribe by showing that they deserve respectful treatment. Fulfilling commitments to the tribe is the ultimate sign of respect that has lasting impacts of trust and the confidence that tribe members will meet their commitments to each other.

Treasure the gift of feedback. One of the servant leader's most uncomfortable responsibilities is to provide redirection to tribe members. Servant leaders don't want to hurt feelings or discourage their people. They are their *coaches*, not their taskmasters. That's a given. But how well do servant leaders receive feedback themselves? Is feedback a gift? Or does it feel more like a shaming incident? Servant leaders must be continuous learners, just as everyone in their tribe must be. And so, sometimes the gift of feedback is an uncomfortable one. Still one to treasure.

Above everything else, love their people. Servant leaders sincerely want the best for their people. And they consider it their purpose to provide the support and resources their people need to perform at their best. When servant leaders love their people, the tribe members know through everyday interactions that they matter and they belong.

I started out this chapter sharing with you two versions of my personal purpose statements. First the 2001 version. And then the latest one. Depending on how far into the future you read this book, I might have revised and refined my life's purpose statement yet again. Maybe even a few more times.

But no matter how many times I review my own life's purpose statement, nothing can compare with Alan Mulally's statement that he wrote in the foreword of a book we both contributed to in 2018, *Work Is Love Made Visible: A Collection of Essays About the Power of Finding Your Purpose from the World's Greatest Thought Leaders.*

This is where the former CEO of Boeing and Ford Motor Company wrote simply, "The purpose of life is to love and be loved, in that order."

The purpose of leadership is to love. And that's where your power truly lies.

BEST: Develop your own personal purpose statement and then seriously look at all the ways your role as a leader empowers you to live out your personal purpose.

WORST: Assume that your title and position on the org chart are all you need to be a leader who achieves results.

FIRST: Read the book *Work Is Love Made Visible.* Don't skip the foreword.

Chapter 24

YOUR LEGACY IS
YOUR ULTIMATE WHY

You've likely already heard this story. But bear with me anyway. It's the one about the three stone masons who are asked by a passerby, "Whatcha doing?" This one question yields three different answers . . .

"I'm carving this rock into blocks," says Stone Mason 1. True enough. But not very inspiring. But that's okay—only three hours left of this heavy labor banging away at the resistant stone before lunchtime. And there's pride in the work: The edges are reliably sharp and straight. The angles are crisp and uniform.

"I'm building a wall," says Stone Mason 2, who clearly understands that there might actually be a purpose associated with all this effort. Keep people in? Keep people out? Who knows? That's above the pay grade. One thing is for sure, it's going to be a very, very good wall, the stone mason says proudly.

"I'm building a cathedral," says the truly visionary Stone Mason 3, who, as they say, understands the assignment. Now, this stone mason knows that the calories burned by such intense physical labor will eventually be transformed into a soaring building complete with spires, flying buttresses, stained glass windows, and an overall uplifting experience for all those—nobility and peasants alike—who have the good fortune to see it upon its completion.

This is the story of the power of vision and purpose. And this is usually where the story concludes. But what if I told you that there is a fourth stone mason who is asked the same question? The conversation goes this way:

Passerby: "Whatcha doing?"

Stone Mason 4: "I'm building the heart of a city that will grow up and around it for centuries. First there will be a grand plaza where farmers and families will meet once a week to trade money for essential nutrition that will support the passing on of DNA far into a distant future. This is where children will watch their parents perform the basic rituals of commerce, which will keep the economic engine of an entire nation humming. Once the plaza is finished, I will then participate in the completion of a breathtaking shrine to the immense privilege of being a part of a greater Plan, where generations after generations of humanity will express their joy and gratitude in timeless music, poetry, wisdom, paintings, sculpture, and prayer. In summary, I am creating a place where happiness and belonging and all the human experiences and emotions can be offered up in gratitude to the generations that follow."

In this progression of conversation, we travel from the concept of a **job**, which, in the case of Stone Mason 1, is quantifiable in units of time, and blocks of stone, with good, strong, sharp planes and edges necessary for eventual stacking. Then we move on to what some might call a **career**, where components of results combine to create a transformative entity, in this case Stone Mason 2's wall, which requires planning, patience, and effort over time where the outcome can be initially described in a sketch, blueprint, plan, recipe, or resume. Then we move on to Stone Mason 3's **calling**, where head, hands, and heart collaborate to manifest the dream that will enable an experience that, presumably, would glorify the human relationship to the universe in an undeniable way. Sure, the blocks must be counted and then assembled. And walls must be erected. Blueprints drawn up. But the emotional outcome remains in the mind's eye and devotion of the creators, designers, builders, until completion. Ideally within the creators' lifetimes. But no promises. Nevertheless, this is their *why*.

But with Stone Mason 4, we're taking all this energy, effort, vision, and sacrifice from hundreds, if not thousands, of devoted artisans over time to create a future outcome that they will most certainly never directly experience themselves. But humanity will benefit. This is the artisans' **legacy**.

Thanks in no small part to Simon Sinek's landmark work *Start with Why*, we leaders are reasonably conversant in the concept of *why*, which, before he came along, was more commonly spoken of in terms of purpose—ideas that fit neatly in Stone Mason 3's experience of *calling*. This is what Simon Sinek refers to as the Just Cause, which is a vision that is so large in scope and flung so far into the future that it's a never-ending quest that people could die trying to achieve. Not that the effort itself will kill the person (though it might), but it is a constantly moving horizon. There is no arriving; there is only the living out of the vision. Which, is, actually, the legacy itself.

Your legacy takes you by the hand and pulls you into a future that is beyond your ability to fully predict or even control. I learned this personally when I received a letter from an audience member a year after a speech I gave about the power of organizational purpose.

As we have already seen, the purpose of WD-40 Company is "to create positive, lasting memories." And that is what I spoke about that day.

Months later I received a note from "Ben," starting with the words, "You probably don't remember me, but . . ." He then told me that as a result of my influence on the stage, he had determined that his employer didn't align with his values. So he left it for a new company and now he couldn't be happier.

But more to the point, and more from the heart, he told me the story of a trip he took to Lowe's with his 10-year-old daughter. Their errand: to buy a can of Multi-Use Product so together they could spruce up his bicycle, starting with the uncooperative chain.

"You know what we just did?" he asked the little girl in the car on the way home. More interested in what was on her phone screen than what was in the shopping bag, she shrugged and simply said, "Bought some oil, I guess."

His response: "No, we just bought a memory."

Later in the garage, the father poured a spot of the oil on a rag and gently extended the rag to the daughter to breathe in that distinctive smell. "You will remember this moment forever," he told her. "Every time you smell WD-40."

Which is only partly correct. She will remember her father forever, and the memory of this moment will spring him back to life in her heart at the most unpredictable moments, whenever there is a whiff of WD-40 in the air. And then she will tell her children, who will then tell their children. And the legacy of Ben and his love for all the future generations will be renewed as year after year a can is taken down from its shelf. The legacy of this father–daughter bike project is one in which he gives her the experience of being needed, of belonging, of being valued, of being welcomed and included. All experiences that she will then pass on to her children. Not a bad legacy, if you ask me.

But the story doesn't end there. His kind note made me think about what my own legacy would be. For years I had identified with the purpose of WD-40 Company, "To create positive, lasting memories." But until I was inspired by his note, I never stopped to think of how that purpose might be transformed into a legacy one day. How nice it would be to one day discover that my commitment to making sure that my tribe—all the people I have had the privilege of knowing and loving throughout my life—would carry with them the certainty that they mattered. And, let's be honest, to know that I mattered too—to them and future generations my influence might inspire.

So let's return for just a moment to that construction project with the four stone masons. Let's choose a real one in particular. And let's choose a time. Back in the 11th century, a small church commenced construction in Dresden, Germany. It wasn't a cathedral quite yet. Just a small church in a small town. But the masons worked year-round in Germany's inhospitable seasons, sweating, freezing, hurting themselves, teaching their children their craft and skills, eventually dying of old age while their children took up the tools and the calling, and taught children of their own. Who in turn passed their skills on to future generations. Century after century, the famed, beloved Frauenkirche rose, transformed, transformed again, and blossomed into the beloved heart of the city, primarily known today by shoppers and tourists for its inimitable china.

Fast-forward to a February night in 1945 and the once grand cathedral was reduced to a mountain of ancient bricks. A series of fire bombings in just a handful of nights had killed more than 25,000 Dresdeners. But the church stood. Until it collapsed from within.

Even though their own lives were torn apart by death, grief, their homes also reduced to rubble, the surviving Dresdeners gathered in the Neumarkt quarter of the city where they saw sky instead of the church's famous dome. Their task: arranging the bricks according to a meticulous plan created to one day help future architects and restorers (most of whom were not even born yet) reconstruct the cathedral. Brick by brick. One day. Eventually. In the unforeseeable, even unpredictable, future.

This was everyone's legacy. Millions of Dresdeners through the centuries embraced the Frauenkirche as their own. But it all started with Stone Mason 1 and the first impact of the first hammer and chisel into the first rough rock.

What is your legacy? And when does it begin?

BEST: Always remember that your actions, reactions, decisions, choices, and behavior will impact not only your day-to-day workplace culture but also families and other workplaces far into the future.

WORST: Assume that who you are and your choices impact only the immediate moment.

FIRST: Think about how you want to influence the way future generations feel about themselves and their prospects for a rewarding, emotionally secure future. Make a list of the behaviors that will directly promote those beliefs far into the future.

Chapter 25

DON'T JUST DRIFT OFF INTO THE VOID

One of the perks of sticking around long enough to be able to look back on many decades of Learning Moments is that you collect wonderful, wise friends along the way. Some whose advice you seek out. Some who will give it to you anyway. I count Marshall Goldsmith as among the former. Whatever he has to tell me, I'm all ears.

One day about eight years ago, I was thinking aloud about eventually retiring from WD-40 Company. Then I asked the question that everyone asks at least once in their life, "And then what?" To which he replied, "Whatever you do, don't just drift off into the void."

Well, that advice stuck in my mind in the form of an image. I immediately envisioned an untethered astronaut drifting helplessly and silently into space, arms and legs spread-eagle, his useless lifeline floating behind him. No one can hear his scream.

Who would want that scenario as their next significant iteration of an inspiring life to be proud of? Most certainly, not I.

But then I thought of the traditional Japanese art form *kintsugi*, roughly translated into English as "golden journey." There is also a void involved in this scenario—instead of the vast emptiness outside the protective space suit, the empty space is contained *within* a vessel that has been pieced together with a network of veins of gold solder. Imagine a beautiful ceramic bowl, masterfully crafted by the artisan, much cherished by its owner. But now in pieces. Then the *kintsugi* artist comes along and reassembles the bowl, attaching the pieces with molten gold. The result? A reimagined bowl, made up of pieces of the past, and made tight, whole, even stronger, more valuable, and certainly more beautiful by the threads of gold. And definitely more interesting.

And the void? It's that valuable space within, ready to accept a new payload of precious cargo. This time, it's made up of intentionally selected items that will make that bowl even more precious, even more beautiful, more useful for its new assignment. And the bowl itself is made slightly larger all around by the expansive gold veining. So, now it's more capacious. That bowl is your new life, your new career, your retirement (or *refirement*, as I like to say). The pieces aren't shards of a broken past, they're components of a past: skills, life experiences, knowledge, relationships, insights that you can redeploy into your next life's bowl. What are you going to put into it?

As much as you might enjoy looking forward to a major, mostly positive change in your life, such as retirement or a career transition, there are some aspects of leaving the old life behind that you might not have prepared yourself for. Indications that not only have you moved beyond your last version of yourself, but that world has also moved beyond you. You have to hand in your key card, maybe sign a stack of papers agreeing to relinquish access or claim to the future. Your email account has vaporized. Your biometrics? No longer recognized by the security system. Your opinions? Maybe not as entirely enthusiastically received by those people who are now working for your successor. As much as you resolve to keep your past company at an emotional arm's length, it still takes longer than you'd like to get used to the fact that big changes are being made—maybe some of your most cherished projects rolled back or canceled altogether—as your successor starts implementing new ideas. No one is asking for your input, let alone permission.

When you travel? Well, that's another set of calculations. You're no longer the celebrated frequent flyer with the key to members-only lounges and hotel floors that only other frequent guests are welcome in. You may still hear friendly flight attendants who remember you call you by name. But eventually they'll move on too. And soon that person taking your boarding pass doesn't know you from the twelve-year-old waiting in line behind you. Boarding Group C? That would be you. You are now just a butt that needs to be buckled into a seat before the plane can take off. And, speaking of butts, the lav is located all the way in the back.

After the parties and tributes have subsided and everyone has returned to their daily lives, you have to figure out the rest for yourself. Hopefully you'll have the support of a coach and a creative, optimistic, possibility-thinking family. But you're still on your own with figuring out the details. No. Correction. For *reinventing* the details. Even better—*reconfiguring* the details, to create what executive coach and author Michael Bungay Stanier calls, in his book *How to Begin*, the Worthy Goal.

The Worthy Goal is the next big project on your horizon. Perhaps you think you're at the time in your life when all the big projects are behind you. And yet, there's that twinkling feeling of ambition—for your own sake or for the world's—that continues to ignite your imagination and elbow its way into your dreams. Once you figure out what it is that keeps tugging at your sleeve with ever-increasing insistence, a new adventure has begun.

"You struggle and stumble, and you also figure it out, learn and grow," Stanier writes. "You build capacity, wisdom, and confidence. You reveal and strengthen your Best Self as you do the work.

"As you unlock your greatness by working on the hard things, you'll make a difference and you'll make the world a little better."

Your Worthy Goal could be the assembly of an entirely different set of skills, social network, and associates to transform yourself and your life's purpose (who says we only get one purpose in life?). Or it can be a rearranging of everything you've done before, all the philosophies you've embraced, all the relationships you've nurtured over time to turbocharge that life mission you've been about all along. That's what I did.

As I began to think about—and then talk about—the answer to my question "And then what?" I started to speak in terms of an apprenticeship. Not an apprenticeship I was about to step into, but the three-plus decades of on-the-job learning I had already done. I had completed my apprenticeship, and am now about the business of taking everything I've learned from experiences and the masters I've been honored to learn from, to do the thing I have been meant to do from the earliest days of my childhood.

To wit: make people happy. In my particular case, to help leaders create workplaces in which people can be happy going to work every day, knowing that their efforts make a contribution to a cause bigger than themselves; where they feel safe, protected, and set free by a compelling set of values; where they learn something new and try different things without fear. As you know, this experience makes people happy. Happy people make happy families. Happy families make happy communities. And finally, happy communities make a happy world.

This continued vision for how I can leverage everything I've been and done before into a future that would keep me excited about moving forward. That's my Worthy Goal. Now how do we go about helping you as you seek out your own? Returning to Stanier's book, he tells us that a Worthy Goal must have three attributes. It must be thrilling, important, and daunting.

- **Thrilling**—You're excited by the germ of the idea of mission. Before the "yeah buts" and the "how do I's" start to weigh you down, you're aloft with the excitement of the possibilities wrapped up in your new goal. How your life will change. The new people you will meet. What you will learn. The new skills you will master. The places you will go. The boundaries and barriers you will gleefully smash. The lives you will change. The fears you will prevail over. The experiences and activities you've long dreamed of but could never quite connect the dots to get you there. The goose bumps. The absence of the word *should*, and how it's replaced with "yes!"

- **Important**—The outcome of your Worthy Goal must be larger than yourself in some way, benefiting the world beyond the boundaries of your own immediate self-interests. Stanier writes, "It's a project or a goal that's for a bigger win than just self-satisfaction or self-gratification. The stakes are higher than your life."

- **Daunting**—The *daunting* attribute forces you to defy your comfort zone. As wise as you might be to leverage all the things you've been and learned in your past, daunting takes you to what Stanier refers to as "the learning edge," that frontier where trying new things ups the ante and potential failure isn't entirely out of the question. But it's temporary failure in service of that thrilling and important mission you have assigned yourself. So take heart.

Are you going to be the drifting astronaut? Or the bowl reassembled with gold? How you make that decision will be your next Learning Moment.

Have fun. Flourish in the void of your choice. Don't hurt anyone. Keep learning. Be happy.

BEST: Welcome each new chapter in your life as an exciting opportunity to fill your life with new adventures, new tribes, new opportunities to make changes in the world that are increasingly meaningful, essential, and undeniable.

WORST: Become so overly identified with your current role, company, companionship of colleagues, stature, and status that you forget to consider the "what then" possibilities. Until it's too late.

FIRST: Resolve to keep the "what then" conversation going, even if it's only in the privacy of your own mind until you build a trusted circle of supporters whose opinions you respect.

Epilogue: Pleasure in the Job Puts Perfection in the Work

I t's remarkable how one otherwise unnoteworthy flight can change the trajectory of a person's career. When I had boarded that Sydney-bound flight, I was a thoughtful, curious, dedicated bloke who had landed the dream assignment to take a wonderful company—and a beloved brand—to the global marketplace. I knew I had the personal responsibility to be worthy of the task and all my colleagues, who would one day enthusiastically call themselves tribe members. And for that responsibility, I knew that I had to keep a beginner's mind and be receptive to all the wisdom that I would be fortunate enough to be exposed to.

Which is how I had the chance to read the Dalai Lama quote: "Our prime purpose in life is to make others happy. And if we can't make them happy, at least don't hurt them." But the wise ones of the ages weren't through with me just yet. Like the spirits in Charles Dickens's *A Christmas Carol*, one more ghost of wisdom past was queued up to pay me an in-flight visit as I could hear the landing gears begin to position themselves for final descent.

This one was from Aristotle. As I put the Dalai Lama's article back in my bag, and pulled out a fresh bit of reading, it was as if the old man reached up through the millennia, gave me a fond cuff on the cheek, much like a favorite uncle might, and said, "Good on ya, Garry. You have done your homework well. Here's one for the road." And then I read the single line that put all my thinking into place. Not only my thoughts from the trip. But also the way I sorted and filtered my leadership forever after.

"Pleasure in the job puts perfection in the work."

A catchy phrase. Just nine words long. As pithy as any jingle that might emerge from modern-day advertising. Even in its brevity, the layers of profound meaning in that one sentence have survived the ages. While I have to admit to being a little surprised by the thought that the ancients were overly concerned with the question "Do I love my job?" the idea of employee engagement was very much on my mind. But I had yet to discover that this question would also apply to me over time when the years-long perspective of the day-to-day performing of the job would eventually transform into a life's work. That would take time. Sitting in my airplane seat, watching the lights of Sydney spread out before me below, I knew even then that making sure that I would deliver a pleasurable job experience to WD-40 Company tribe members would be my life's work.

And they, in turn, would one day hold the same philosophy for those who looked to *them* for leadership.

Pleasure. Perfection. What could these words have meant to a philosopher knocking around Greece between 384 and 322 BC? I suppose anyone, no matter when they lived, would agree that *perfection* is about as absolute a value as you can get. Maybe there might be some disagreement as to what perfection in any single thing under consideration might be. I'll leave that to people smarter than I.

Pleasure. Now that's an ideal subject to interpretation, experience, and even the level of maturity of the person who is seeking it. From a leader's perspective, when we understand the kind of pleasure we want to promise our tribe members, we also understand more clearly what kinds of tribe members we want to attract and invite into our community. Employers learned the hard way, for instance, in the early 2000s, that the offer of PlayStations, margarita machines, and foosball tables only attracted employees who wanted those kinds of things on the job. There was pleasure in the play but not in the work itself. So, that didn't work, did it? At least not for very long.

Naturally, the fun and celebrations that come with the tribe experience at WD-40 Company are an essential part of their careers there. Our celebrations and fun times had one prime objective—to create a positive, lasting memory of our time together that would remind us of the importance of connection and appreciation, and reinforce the principle that we are a place where people belong and really do matter. If you know any Aussies, you know we are pretty good at creating a good party so I will leave it to your imagination. Hard work can go hand in hand with the lighthearted spirit.

As I sat buckled into my plane seat with tray table up, I imagined what pleasure might generate the perfection of the experience of working at WD-40 Company for the hundreds of tribe members who chose to cast their lot with us. And this is what I came up with, which has since been honed and polished over the years:

"Pleasure in a job is made up of affirmative answers to these questions: 'Am I loved?' 'Am I acknowledged?' 'Am I seen to be doing my best work?' And, 'Is the person who is coaching or leading me not only loving me up but also brave enough to be able to help me be my best self?'"

The pleasure side is more about the love and acknowledgment and knowing that one matters. It's the action around the redirection and the coaching that increases competency, which then contributes to the perfection in the work. Consequently, the coach must be tough-minded and tenderhearted at times. But always in the context of having the individual's best interests in mind, as well as the needs of the company.

As the years began to pile up, I discovered that while it was my job (honor, actually) to provide those kinds of pleasures to WD-40 Company tribe members, I also needed that same experience myself in order to have what was necessary to put perfection in my work. I've heard it said about the nature of a career in leadership: "It's a personal development program wrapped in a career opportunity." As it turns out, the personal journey of being a leader is also a journey to a better self as well as a better community of tribe members dedicated to protecting and feeding one another.

The pleasure and perfection (to whatever extent might have been within my reach on any given day) came for me because I saw that what I was doing was worthwhile. It wasn't just worthwhile because we were creating substantial wealth for a bunch of shareholders. It was more rewarding because we were creating an environment, a culture where people enjoyed what they did.

I like to say to audiences I speak to, "Imagine a place where you go to work each day, make a contribution to something bigger than yourself, learn something new, protected and set free by a compelling set of values. And then go home happy."

It's an ideal vision, to be sure. But I think I pulled it off, while serving shareholders at the same time. In fact, I don't think we would have filled the coffers of shareholders if people weren't doing the work that they were doing and enjoying it, having fun, and learning in the company of people they truly considered to be their friends. All pulling for one another.

Creating that environment was, to me, the source of pleasure in my job. The privilege of watching people develop and then turning around to help those coming up behind them became the perfection of my work. Grace, who is the country manager of China, started as an administrative assistant. Shannon started as a part-time receptionist and now leads the sales team for Walmart. Meghan began as a lab assistant. After returning to school and obtaining her PhD, she became our global leader of R&D. And the company has sent more than 30 tribe members through the same MSEL program with Ken Blanchard that gave me my own leadership start so many years ago when I first landed in the United States.

At this writing, I can proudly say that I have just completed the 25 years of my apprenticeship in leadership.

Now, it's time to put what I've learned to work. Any dumb-ass can do it.

Recommended Reading

The Advice Trap: Be Humble, Stay Curious & Change the Way You Lead Forever, Michael Bungay Stanier (Page Two Books, 2020)

All I Really Need to Know I Learned in Kindergarten: Uncommon Thoughts on Common Things, Robert Fulghum (Ballantine Books, 2004)

Anxiety at Work: 8 Strategies to Help Teams Build Resilience, Handle Uncertainty, and Get Stuff Done, Adrian Gostick and Chester Elton (Harper Business, 2021)

Build an A-Team: Play to Their Strengths and Lead Them Up the Learning Curve, Whitney Johnson (Harvard Business Review Press, 2018)

The Coaching Habit: Say Less, Ask More & Change the Way You Lead Forever, Michael Bungay Stanier (Page Two, 2016)

Counselling for Toads: A Psychological Adventure, Robert de Board (Routledge, 1997)

Crucial Conversations: Tools for Talking When Stakes Are High, Joseph Grenny, Kerry Patterson, Ron McMillan, Al Switzler, and Emily Gregory (McGraw-Hill, 2002)

Disrupt Yourself: Master Relentless Change and Speed Up Your Learning Curve, Whitney Johnson (Harvard Business Review Press, 2019)

The Earned Life: Lose Regret, Choose Fulfillment, Marshall Goldsmith and Mark Reiter (Crown Currency, 2022)

Engage!: How WD-40 Company Built the Engine of Positive Culture, Stan Sewitch (Trafford Publishing, 2023)

Everybody Matters: The Extraordinary Power of Caring for Your People Like Family, Bob Chapman and Raj Sisodia (Portfolio, 2015)

Flourish: A Visionary New Understanding of Happiness and Well-Being, Martin Seligman (Atria Books, 2012)

Focus: The Future of Your Company Depends on It, Alan Ries (Harper Business, 1996)

Healing at Work: A Guide to Using Career Conflicts to Overcome Your Past and Build the Future You Deserve, Susan Schmitt Winchester and Martha I. Finney (Telemachus Press, 2021)

The Heart of Business: Leadership Principles for the Next Era of Capitalism, Hubert Joly and Caroline Lambert (Harvard Business Review Press, 2021)

Helping People Win at Work: A Business Philosophy Called "Don't Mark My Paper, Help Me Get an A," Ken Blanchard and Garry Ridge (Pearson, 2009)

How to Begin: Start Doing Something That Matters, Michael Bungay Stanier (Page Two, 2022)

HR from the Heart: Inspiring Stories and Strategies for Building the People Side of Great Business, Libby Sartain and Martha I. Finney (Amacom Books, 2003)

The Infinite Game: Simon Sinek (Portfolio, 2019)

Leaders Eat Last: Why Some Teams Pull Together and Others Don't, Simon Sinek (Portfolio, 2014)

The Leadership Challenge: How to Make Extraordinary Things Happen in Organizations, James M. Kouzes and Barry Z. Posner (Jossey-Bass, 2023)

Leading at a Higher Level: Blanchard on Leadership and Creating High Performing Organizations, Kenneth Blanchard (FT Press, 2018)

Leading with Gratitude: Eight Leadership Practices for Extraordinary Business Results, Chester Elton and Adrian Gostick (Harper Business, 2020)

Legacy: What the All Blacks Can Teach Us About the Business of Life, James Kerr (Constable & Robinson, 2013)

Loonshots: How to Nurture the Crazy Ideas That Win Wars, Cure Diseases, and Transform Industries, Safi Bahcall (Griffin, 2020)

Multipliers: How the Best Leaders Make Everyone Smarter, Liz Wiseman (Harper Business, 2017)

The New One Minute Manager: Ken Blanchard and Spencer Johnson (William Morrow, 2015)

Out of the Maze: An A-Mazing Way to Get Unstuck, Spencer Johnson (Portfolio, 2018)

Right Kind of Wrong: The Science of Failing Well, Amy Edmondson (Simon and Schuster, 2023)

Shackleton's Way: Leadership Lessons from the Great Antarctic Explorer, Margot Morrell and Stephanie Capparell (Penguin Books, 2002)

Simple Truths of Leadership: 52 Ways to Be a Servant Leader and Build Trust, Ken Blanchard and Randy Conley (Berrett-Koehler, 2022)

Start with Why: How Great Leaders Inspire Everyone to Take Action, Simon Sinek (Portfolio, 2009)

Survive, Reset, Thrive: Leading Breakthrough Growth Strategy in Volatile Times, Rebecca Homkes (Kogan Page, 2024)

Teaming: How Organizations Learn, Innovate, and Compete in the Knowledge Economy, Amy Edmondson (Jossey-Bass Pfeiffer, 2012)

The Tipping Point: How Little Things Can Make a Big Difference, Malcolm Gladwell (Little, Brown, 2000)

To Be Honest: Lead with the Power of Truth, Justice and Purpose, Ron Carucci (Kogan Page, 2021)

Tribe: On Homecoming and Belonging, Sebastian Junger (Twelve, 2016)

Triggers: Creating Behavior That Lasts—Becoming the Person You Want to Be, Marshall Goldsmith and Mark Reiter (Crown Currency, 2015)

Trust Works!: Four Keys to Building Lasting Relationships, Ken Blanchard, Cynthia Olmstead, and Martha Lawrence (William Morrow, 2013)

The Truth About Getting the Best from People: Ditch the Carrot and the Stick, Martha I. Finney (FT Press, 2012)

Turn the Ship Around!: A True Story of Turning Followers into Leaders, David Marquet (Penguin Books, 2019)

The Unlocked Leader: Dare to Free Your Own Voice, Lead with Empathy, and Shine Your Light in the World, Hortense le Gentil and Caroline Lambert (Wiley, 2023)

The Vision Code: How to Create and Execute a Compelling Vision for Your Business, Oleg Konovalov (Wiley, 2021)

What Got You Here Won't Get You There: How Successful People Become Even More Successful, Marshall Goldsmith and Mark Reiter (Hachette Books, 2007)

Who Moved My Cheese?: An A-Mazing Way to Deal with Change in Your Work and in Your Life, Spencer Johnson (Ebury Publishing, 2009)

Why Motivating People Doesn't Work . . . and What Does: More Break-throughs for Leading, Energizing, and Engaging, Susan Fowler (Berrett-Koehler, 2023)

Work Is Love Made Visible: A Collection of Essays About the Power of Finding Your Purpose from the World's Greatest Thought Leaders, Frances Hesselbein, Marshall Goldsmith, and Sarah McArthur (Wiley, 2018)

You, Me, We: Why We All Need a Friend at Work (and How to Show Up as One!), Morag Barrett, Eric Spencer, and Ruby Vesely (Page Two, 2022)

Acknowledgments

To everyone who has played a role in my journey, I extend my deepest gratitude.

First, to the amazing team at WD-40 Company, your dedication, creativity, and relentless pursuit of excellence have made this journey not only successful but also incredibly rewarding.

To every member of the WD-40 Company tribe, your willingness to embrace the principles of servant leadership and your commitment to creating a culture of learning and innovation have been truly inspiring.

To my coauthor, Martha Finney, thank you for your partnership, insights, and unwavering support. Your ability to capture the essence of our work and bring it to life in these pages is nothing short of remarkable. Thank you to Mark Christensen for introducing us so many years ago, which launched an epic writing partnership of nearly a decade.

My thanks also go to the entire team who collaborated to bring *Any Dumb-Ass Can Do It* to reality. Jim Levine, my literary agent. And the talented tribe at BenBella Books: Matt Holt, Katie

Dickman, Lydia Choi, Mallory Hyde, Brigid Pearson, Jessika Rieck, Kerri Stebbins, and Ariel Jewett.

To Ken Blanchard, your mentorship and friendship have been invaluable. Your teachings on leadership have profoundly shaped my approach and have been a cornerstone of our success.

Likewise, to all the leaders and thinkers whose work has influenced and inspired me, your contributions to the field of leadership and organizational culture are deeply appreciated.

A special thanks to my family and friends for their love, patience, and understanding. Your support has been my anchor, allowing me to pursue my passion and make a positive and lasting difference in the lives of others.

And finally, to every reader who picks up this book, thank you for your interest and commitment to becoming a better leader. I hope the lessons and insights shared here will help you create a culture where people are inspired to be their best selves.

About the Authors

Garry Ridge—The Culture Coach

Founder of The Learning Moment, www.thelearningmoment.net
Chairman Emeritus, WD-40 Company
Marshall Goldsmith Certified Executive Coach
Named Among Top 10 Most Admired CEOs in the World—*Inc.*
  magazine
Global Gurus 2024 Top 30 Organizational Culture #2
LeadersHum Power List 2023 of the Biggest Voices in Leadership
  #12

Photo by Ted Saunders
(Tedshots.com)

Garry Ridge spent 25 years as CEO building one of the world's most beloved and recognized brands—WD-40 Company—starting with creating a culture of leaders and individual contributors who are genuinely joyful in their work. He refers to this time of his career as his apprenticeship. And now, he fulfills his life's purpose by transforming his learnings into teachings, extending his guidance as a coach to companies and executives worldwide.

Garry coauthored *Helping People Win at Work* with Ken Blanchard and contributed a chapter to the Marshall Goldsmith / Frances Hesselbein book *Work Is Love Made Visible*.

As part of his lifelong commitment to helping others develop, Garry is an adjunct professor at the University of San Diego. He also serves on the Gorilla Glue Company Advisory Board and Eastridge Workforce Solutions board.

Garry's ideal coaching clients have these attributes in common: (1) A sincere desire to create a workplace environment that promotes psychological safety, belonging, and happiness in the work. (2) An eagerness to replace ego with empathy. (3) The characteristics of humble servant leadership as their starting place.

"Creating a workplace experience where people gather as a tribe, where they support, protect, nurture each other, is simple, but not easy," he says. "This goal is within anyone's reach. You have to want it absolutely more than the typical rewards that come with the usual C-suite. More than status, elitism, division, all those usual things we find in companies that want to enjoy the benefits of tribal culture but don't want to sacrifice the ego amenities."

If I can accomplish one thing, it would be to help companies create a workplace where people can go to work every day knowing that their efforts make a contribution to a cause bigger than themselves, where they feel safe, protected, and set free every day by a compelling set of values, learn something new, and try new things without fear. This makes happy people. And happy people create happy families and communities. Happy communities create a happy world. And we need a happy world.

Martha Finney

In addition to collaborating with Garry Ridge as his longtime writing partner, Martha has written, coauthored, and ghostwritten 30 books on employee engagement, leadership, career management, and mental health in the workplace. Her books have been published by Simon & Schuster, Amacom (now HarperCollins), Pfeiffer, and FT Press. Her book *The Truth About Getting the Best from People* (FT Press, 2012) has been published in at least five languages. Her 2003 book, coauthored with Libby Sartain, about the culture experience at Southwest Airlines, *HR from the Heart: Inspiring Stories and Strategies for Building the People Side of Great Business*, remains a cherished HR classic today.

Her original research into joy in the American workplace has been featured on CNN, NPR, in *Time* magazine, and major city newspapers such as the *San Jose Mercury News*, the *Miami Herald*, the *San Francisco Chronicle*, and the *New York Post*.

Learn more about Martha at www.Marthafinney.global.